GRAY MATTERS

GRAY MATTERS

The Workplace Survival Guide

Bob Rosner
Allan Halcrow
John Lavin

WILEY

John Wiley & Sons, Inc.

Published by John Wiley & Sons, Inc., Hoboken, New Jersey.
Published simultaneously in Canada.

For general information on our other products and services please contact our Customer Care Department within the United States at (800) 762-2974, outside the United States at (317) 572-3993 or fax (317) 572-4002.

Wiley also publishes its books in a variety of electronic formats. Some content that appears in print may not be available in electronic books. For more information about Wiley products, visit our web site at www.wiley.com.

ISBN: 0-471-45508-3

Printed in the United States of America

10 9 8 7 6 5 4 3 2 1

contents

about the authors

Bob Rosner is a Seattle-based columnist, speaker, author, Webmaster, and workplace commentator. He writes the internationally syndicated column "Working Wounded," and is coauthor of the *Wall Street Journal* best-seller *The Boss's Survival Guide* (McGraw Hill, 2001) and *Working Wounded: Advice that Adds Insight to Injury* (Warner, 2000). As a keynote presenter, he has spoken humorously and memorably to corporations and associations in England, Scotland, Canada, Australia, New Zealand, Argentina, the Philippines, and across the United States. He's the founder of the award-winning WorkingWounded.com. Rosner has been a consultant to *Fortune* 500 companies and government agencies, has founded three corporations, and has served as an adjunct professor to MBA students. He's been interviewed by *People, Good Morning America,* and NPR. Like most of the rest of us, he's taken a bullet or two in the course of his career. You can reach Bob at bob@workingwounded.com or http://graymattersbook.com.

Allan Halcrow is a writer and consultant. He is a partner in WorkPositive, a training and consulting firm that focuses on interpersonal skills in the workplace. Clients include Lucas Digital, Pfizer, McKesson, Stanford Hotels, Teradyne, and the Metropolitan Water District. He is coauthor of the *Wall Street Journal* best-seller *The Boss's Survival Guide* (McGraw-Hill, July 2001). Allan is the former publisher and editor-in-chief of *Workforce* (formerly *Personnel Journal*). His work as a journalist has been recognized with the McAllister Editorial Fellowship from the American Business Press and awards from the American Society of Business Press Editors and the Western Publications Association. He is based in Irvine, California. You can reach Allan at ahalcrow@workpositive.com.

John Lavin is an artist in Seattle. He recently learned that many bookstores have a whole section dedicated to books about business. You can reach John via Lavinstacey@hotmail.com.

about the authors

Bob Rosner is a Seattle-based columnist, speaker, author, Webmaster, and workplace commentator. He writes the internationally syndicated column "Working Wounded," and is coauthor of the *Wall Street Journal* best-seller *The Boss's Survival Guide* (McGraw Hill, 2001) and *Working Wounded: Advice that Adds Insight to Injury* (Warner, 2000). As a keynote presenter, he has spoken humorously and memorably to corporations and associations in England, Scotland, Canada, Australia, New Zealand, Argentina, the Philippines, and across the United States. He's the founder of the award-winning WorkingWounded.com. Rosner has been a consultant to *Fortune* 500 companies and government agencies, has founded three corporations, and has served as an adjunct professor to MBA students. He's been interviewed by *People, Good Morning America,* and NPR. Like most of the rest of us, he's taken a bullet or two in the course of his career. You can reach Bob at bob@workingwounded.com or http://graymattersbook.com.

Allan Halcrow is a writer and consultant. He is a partner in WorkPositive, a training and consulting firm that focuses on interpersonal skills in the workplace. Clients include Lucas Digital, Pfizer, McKesson, Stanford Hotels, Teradyne, and the Metropolitan Water District. He is coauthor of the *Wall Street Journal* best-seller *The Boss's Survival Guide* (McGraw-Hill, July 2001). Allan is the former publisher and editor-in-chief of *Workforce* (formerly *Personnel Journal*). His work as a journalist has been recognized with the McAllister Editorial Fellowship from the American Business Press and awards from the American Society of Business Press Editors and the Western Publications Association. He is based in Irvine, California. You can reach Allan at ahalcrow@workpositive.com.

John Lavin is an artist in Seattle. He recently learned that many bookstores have a whole section dedicated to books about business. You can reach John via Lavinstacey@hotmail.com.

acknowledgments

Thanks to everyone who has written me through the years or has contributed to Working-Wounded.com or attended one of my Retention Evangelist seminars. Your insight and creativity are a constant source of inspiration. Thanks to Gail Ross, the best darn agent in the world. Thanks to the entire Wiley family, especially Micheline Frederick. Thanks to United Media and all of the papers and Web sites that run Working Wounded. Thanks to my family and friends. Thanks to Dave Gray for being there in the beginning. Thanks to Annie Barrett, who introduced us to John Lavin, a remarkably creative spirit and colleague. Finally, it's a blessing to be able to collaborate with Allan Halcrow, who never knew he had all these characters living inside his head.

—BR

My great thanks to Brian Gillet, sounding board, critic, and unyielding support; I could not do it without you. I also want to thank my sister, Cheryl Halcrow, for being a great friend and inspiration. I am blessed to have two great business partners, Nancy Breuer and Lynne Gabriel; thank you for the joy you bring to my life and work. Thanks to John (for making the characters real) and especially to Bob, for giving me a second act and forcing me to accept that I'm a writer. Thank you, too, to Douglas and Eileen Halcrow, Shari Caudron, Linda Davidson, Juanita Odin, and Charlene Solomon for being there. Thank you to Gail Ross and Airie Stuart for helping make an unconventional idea a reality. And last, but never least: thanks to my nieces, Marie and Nathalie, for about a million reasons.

—AH

I'd like to thank Carrie Stacey, whose love, critical eye, and hard work made this possible. Thanks also to Page and Petra for being such good sports and great kids. Thanks to the Lavins and the Staceys for all the support while the project was under way. Thanks to Jenny and Janos for picking up the slack, and to Winfield for keeping me in line. Special thanks to Annie Barrett for the introduction to the project, and for watching out for me. And thanks to Bob and Allan for their remarkable generosity.

—JL

acknowledgments

Thanks to everyone who has written me through the years or has contributed to Working-Wounded.com or attended one of my Retention Evangelist seminars. Your insight and creativity are a constant source of inspiration. Thanks to Gail Ross, the best darn agent in the world. Thanks to the entire Wiley family, especially Micheline Frederick. Thanks to United Media and all of the papers and Web sites that run Working Wounded. Thanks to my family and friends. Thanks to Dave Gray for being there in the beginning. Thanks to Annie Barrett, who introduced us to John Lavin, a remarkably creative spirit and colleague. Finally, it's a blessing to be able to collaborate with Allan Halcrow, who never knew he had all these characters living inside his head.

—BR

My great thanks to Brian Gillet, sounding board, critic, and unyielding support; I could not do it without you. I also want to thank my sister, Cheryl Halcrow, for being a great friend and inspiration. I am blessed to have two great business partners, Nancy Breuer and Lynne Gabriel; thank you for the joy you bring to my life and work. Thanks to John (for making the characters real) and especially to Bob, for giving me a second act and forcing me to accept that I'm a writer. Thank you, too, to Douglas and Eileen Halcrow, Shari Caudron, Linda Davidson, Juanita Odin, and Charlene Solomon for being there. Thank you to Gail Ross and Airie Stuart for helping make an unconventional idea a reality. And last, but never least: thanks to my nieces, Marie and Nathalie, for about a million reasons.

—AH

I'd like to thank Carrie Stacey, whose love, critical eye, and hard work made this possible. Thanks also to Page and Petra for being such good sports and great kids. Thanks to the Lavins and the Staceys for all the support while the project was under way. Thanks to Jenny and Janos for picking up the slack, and to Winfield for keeping me in line. Special thanks to Annie Barrett for the introduction to the project, and for watching out for me. And thanks to Bob and Allan for their remarkable generosity.

—JL

introduction

Two lessons: (1) In all things, remember, mind over matter; (2) There is no such thing as a solo career. That's what I always tell people when they ask me what I've learned during the last couple of years at Global Gadget. I've told a lot of people, too, because what we did attracted a lot of attention.

You probably already know our story, but let me fill you in just in case. Global Gadget is a medium-size manufacturing outfit. We make all kinds of gadgets, doohickeys, and thingamajigs and sell them to other manufacturers and to distributors. My name is Gray Blanderson, and I've worked at Global Gadget for a long time. I started out as a summer intern while I was in school, and then when I graduated I went to work as an engineer. I design a lot of the gadgets that we sell.

There are many different kinds of gadgets, so our company has several divisions. I work in our Appliance Division. We make gadgets that get used as parts in various appliances. Our division has never been the biggest or most important in the company, but we have always turned at least a modest profit. I can't say that anything happening at work was too exciting, but it was steady.

One morning we all came to work and it became *very* exciting. The head of our division, Virginia Edgarly, told us that Global Gadget was reorganizing. Specifically, the company was taking the Appliance Division and splitting it in two. One division would produce gadgets for large appliances, such as refrigerators and washing machines. The other division would focus on gadgets for small appliances, such as blenders and hair dryers.

That sounds pretty simple, but it was plenty complicated for us. Top management decided to staff the new Large Appliance Division almost entirely with people from other parts of the company. Those of us who had been the core of the Appliance Division were left to run the new Small Appliance Division. There was one really big challenge in that plan: Gadgets for large appliances accounted for about 80 percent of our revenue and most of our profit. That meant that the new division contributed very little revenue and almost no profit to the company. The situation was so bleak that most experts predicted that our division wouldn't survive six months.

As it turns out, six months is exactly how long we had. Virginia told us the company expected to see dramatic improvement in our numbers by the end of six months or the division would be sold or shut down. Either way, we were suddenly fighting for our survival.

Serious Threats Are Also Great Teachers.

To say that the announcement upended our world is an understatement. *Everything* changed over the next few months: our jobs, our relationships with each other, our products, our business model, and even our workflow. Nothing is the same now, and that's good.

My wife, Taupe, reads a lot of self-help books. One of her favorites is *The Road Less Traveled* by M. Scott Peck. She quotes it to me a lot. That book begins, "Life is difficult." Is it ever! Life is difficult and so is business. Getting through these last months has been really tough, and often painful. But we accomplished a lot and surprised a lot of people. Because of that, people have sought to learn from us.

We've learned so much, and I was spending so much time talking about it, that I finally decided to put it in a book. These two business writers, Bob Rosner and Allan Halcrow, were snooping around here a lot so I asked them to help me. As you'll see, this story isn't all about me. It was a team effort, and I wanted to be sure the whole team got included. That's why we found an artist, John Lavin, to draw what happened—so you could see how things played out and what other people did. The book is based on a journal I kept throughout our turnaround, plus interviews with the others and documents I kept.

What we learned really does fill a whole book, but as I said, there are two main lessons I want to share: (1) In all things, remember, mind over matter; (2) There is no such thing as a solo career.

I've thought a lot about how to explain what I mean. Let me start with a visual image. Turn the page. (Yes, really!) What do you see?

What did you see? A large black dot, right? What else? No, that isn't a trick question. How about the white space around the dot? In business, the white space—the stuff you can't see—is often more important than what you can see.

What You Can't See Affects Every Element of Your Job.

Let me give you an example. Toward the beginning of our turnaround effort, I met Mavis for lunch one day at a local restaurant. (Mavis takes care of my kids, but as you'll see, she's much more than just a babysitter.) I was talking about the stuff happening at Global Gadget, and Mavis crumpled a napkin and threw it on the floor. I started to ask her what she was doing, but she motioned me to be quiet and watch.

The first person who walked by didn't even notice the napkin. I didn't think the second person noticed, either, until she took a busboy aside and pointed at the napkin; when she walked away he went back to what he was doing. He might have come to pick it up eventually, but then another person walked by and he picked it up and threw it in the laundry bin.

Mavis asked me what I could tell about the people we had watched. I didn't have anything brilliant to say, but I mumbled that I would prefer not to work with the first two. "None of us would," Mavis said. "But most of us do." Then she explained that the first person had acted like a typical employee—doing his job but nothing more. The next person was thinking like a typical manager—spotting what needs to be done and then delegating the task to the person who is "supposed to" be doing it. The third person—who actually picked up the napkin—was acting like an owner. "Not everyone can own the company, but we all can show a little more ownership where we work," Mavis said.

Mind over matter. The napkin was plainly visible to everyone. *Attitudes* about the napkin are invisible, but you can see how important they are. If everyone who works at the restaurant acts like an employee, it won't be long until there are a lot of napkins on the floor. If everyone acts like the manager, more time will be spent directing than doing, and everyone will be more focused on each other than they are on the diners. But if everyone acts like an owner, then the whole restaurant will run better.

That said, here's a disclaimer: I'm not going to tell you to work harder or put in more hours. The world has enough people telling you to do that. Like you, if I hear "doing more with less" one more time I'm going to stick my head into the office shredder. *More* is not the answer to anything. But I have learned that when you are a match for the company and the company is a match for you, you've got to accept some ownership for what you do and how you do it.

You Are the Owner of Your Job, Your Attitude, and Your Future.

I sure didn't start out that way, and neither did most of my colleagues. I've got to be honest: We were all stepping over a lot of napkins. I was never really sure if it was a Tuesday or a Thursday and the clock just crawled toward 5 o'clock each day. And yet I can remember telling a coworker once that I was too busy to learn.

There's nothing like facing your own workplace extinction to make you find the time. Mind over matter: I could see that brainpower was our only hope. We had nothing else to draw on. We had very little time. We had no resources. We had no support and no one who really believed in us. We had two choices: figure something out or give up. I wasn't willing to just give up.

It turns out that figuring something out meant figuring a lot of things out. I started out hoping for one catchall answer to our problems, and I learned there was no such thing. Instead, our race against the clock was more like a high-stakes game of chess. If our ultimate goal was checkmate, first we had to get our pawns out of the way. Then, just as in chess, we had to figure out how to best use our pieces—each with its unique capabilities. We also had to learn to anticipate the next moves by our own senior management and our customers. Finally, we had to learn to respond quickly when those moves were surprises. Throughout the months we worked to save the division, we often stopped doing, but we never stopped thinking.

That's one reason we decided to call this book *Gray Matters.* In today's business world, nothing is more important than our gray matter. Nothing. I didn't reach that conclusion just looking at our experience. Think about your own workplace. When is the last time you solved a problem *without* brainpower?

In Business Today, We Have No Greater Resource than Our Own Gray Matter.

It's not such a crazy question. In addition to self-help books, Taupe likes to read history. She likes to talk about what she reads, and a lot of it is pretty interesting. Back when people were still hunting and gathering, problems were usually solved through brute strength and endurance. Strength and endurance were key in agrarian societies, too. In the industrial age, the thing you needed most was capital. If you had capital, you could buy equipment, raw material, and labor. Consider the sweatshops and machine work of that time; no one was paid to think.

Now we're in the information age, which is all about data and how we use it. In theory, we're all paid to think. At some level, companies know this. You can tell because they keep asking their employees to be better educated. Most of the tools we use (from computers to calculators to PDAs) are intended to help us think better.

But in other ways, I don't think most companies *do* get it. Taupe and I talked about it one night over dinner. She pointed out that the basic corporate structure most companies use today was created during the Industrial Revolution. She says it was really created to serve a different kind of economy. I never would have thought of that (I'm not what you would call a thinker), but what she said made a lot of sense. I can sure see that at Global Gadget, and at the companies that we were trying to partner with.

All these companies *say* they want new ideas and creative thinking. But the structures in place are intended to keep ideas under control, not to unleash them. If you doubt it, think about whose approval you need before you are allowed to implement an idea. Yes, I realize that if every new idea were just implemented we would have chaos. But shouldn't management be trying to figure out how to use as many ideas as possible, not how to keep control?

If companies really valued creativity and thinking, wouldn't they pay for them? Instead, they pay for seniority and experience. If they really valued creativity and thinking, they would compensate people for the problems they solved and the ideas they had instead of the hours they worked. These are pretty radical ideas. I got pretty excited talking about them, and Taupe hissed at me that the other people in the restaurant were staring.

I guess I've become sort of an evangelist because I've seen how it can work. We really made things a lot better, but I admit that we were fortunate. We were able to do it because no one got in our way. Management had basically given up on our division, so no one was really paying attention to what we were doing. Even Virginia spent more time focused on the new Large Appliance Division than on ours, so we were free to try whatever we wanted to try. It's funny, isn't it, that the company had to decide that there was nothing left to lose before we were really allowed to give it our all?

Focus on Nurturing and Unleashing Brainpower, Not Keeping It under Control.

So far I've been talking about brainpower as if it were all about linear thinking and problem solving. But there's much more to it than that. Our emotions and intuition are also gray matters. We can learn to use them effectively to strengthen our linear thinking, or we can manage them poorly and undermine our best thinking.

Some people dismiss that as "touchy-feely" stuff. But Taupe told me that a lot of research by Daniel Goleman and other experts shows that emotional intelligence can be a greater predictor of job success than IQ. I'm sure you know people who are very intelligent but don't do well at work because they don't get along well with others. You probably also know some people who aren't the smartest but do very well because they work effectively with others.

We sure saw the importance of that "touchy-feely" stuff. Even with the pressure we faced to get results fast, anger, fatigue, and our own personality quirks still sidetracked us. Working through those issues became so important, in fact, that we started calling them the Seven Deadly Workplace Sins.

We're still sinners from time to time, and we're human so we probably always will be. But we have made great progress. Now we recognize the issues and we have learned to work through the emotions instead of pretending they aren't there.

None of us are born being great people people; emotional intelligence is a learned skill. Extroverts may have a leg up on the rest of us, but even they have to learn empathy, emotional self-awareness, and other abilities. As you read, I'm sure it won't take you long to figure out which skills the team members need to develop, or to see that I need to improve my assertiveness.

Mind over matter. You can't inventory a team's brainpower or emotional skills, but in a crisis they are what matter most.

Your Gray Matter Includes Your Emotional Intelligence. Use It Wisely.

Notice that I referred to a *team's* brainpower and emotional skills. That brings me to my second key point: There is no such thing as a solo career. We really are all in this together. Actually, there's a direct correlation between brainpower and the importance of teams. The sad truth is that none of us is smart enough alone. We need the skills, talents, and even personality quirks of the rest of the team.

Few of us get to choose the people we work with—others do that for us. What we can choose is how we work with those people. I'm not saying you have to like everyone you work with; you won't. But you do have to work with them. I've seen firsthand that investing energy in negativity gets you nowhere. Your mind doesn't have greater than 100 percent capacity. Use your full capacity to find ways to get the most out of your relationship with the rest of the team, not to complain about one weak link. If that means that one person on the team only gets 2 percent of your energy, so be it. But if your team is really functioning well together, the members will work to build strengths in each other so there are no weak links.

I've learned something valuable from every single one of my teammates. Can you say that? I know that without any one of us, we wouldn't have accomplished all that we did. Of course, that didn't just happen by itself. We worked hard at working with each other and figuring out how to use our complementary skills. We didn't always succeed. Sometimes we drove each other crazy.

Sometimes the lessons were painful. I feel like I've had every single one of my flaws dissected over the past few months. It's tough to find out what people really think of you. But I could see that if we were to succeed I had to focus on what was best for the team—and therefore for the company—and not worry so much about my own ego.

That's easier said than done. I know. Companies haven't fully recognized the importance of teamwork, either. They *say* they value teamwork, and heaven help you if you are not perceived as a "team player." But if companies really valued teamwork, then they would evaluate people— and pay them—in teams, instead of as individuals.

I've become kind of an evangelist about teamwork, too, because I've seen that it works. We are the proof of that.

None of Us Alone Is Smart Enough. We Need the Rest of the Team.

Listen to yourself talk about your company. Do you describe your company as "we" and "us" or as "they" and "them"? I used to say "them," and now I always say "we." That's an important shift. It's dumb to spend 8, 9, or 10 hours a day in service of "they" and "them." The crazy thing is that we are often our own worst enemy. We have the chance to become part of something and we don't grab it.

So what did I learn from the experiences that make up this book? I learned how business really works. I learned how to get our sales process on track. I leaned to repent the Seven Deadly Workplace Sins, and I learned the key to innovation. But the most important thing I learned is that you can take two problems and create one solution. Life is difficult, and work is *really* difficult. But if we pull together we can find meaning and community at work.

I once heard that a big corporation spent millions of dollars to determine what was most important to people. They summarized the results in two words: simplicity and control. To that I'd add community. Simplicity, control, and community. If we use our gray matters—*all* our gray matters—we can have it all. Read on. . . .

Gray Blanderson

http://graymattersbook.com

setting the scene

Welcome to Central City, somewhere in America. SUVs fill the parking lot. Teens hang out at the local mall. Parents socialize at their kids' soccer matches. People work, pay their taxes, and watch *Survivor*. But there's trouble in paradise.

Our hero, Gray Blanderson, works for Global Gadget, a maker of complex gadgetry of all sorts. Global's gadgets can be found as components in large industrial equipment, toys, cars, and other products. For a long time, Gray's department has produced gadgets that were used in both large home appliances (such as refrigerators) and small ones (such as vacuums and blenders). But as the story opens, Senior Vice President Virginia Edgarly has just announced a reorganization. Responsibility for gadgets for larger appliances has been moved to a newly created division, leaving Gray's team with responsibility only to the small appliance market. The idea is to increase Global's market share in that area. But the immediate result is that Gray's group has become the smallest, least profitable, and least important division in the company. Everyone knows that without a dramatic turnaround the division could be sold off or closed.

A turnaround won't be easy. Competitors are breathing down Global Gadget's neck. And Gray's division lacks the leadership it needs. Gray decides to step up to the plate and lead the turnaround, but is he up to the task?

Gray Blanderson

Mild-mannered product designer. He's overworked, stressed, and often bewildered. He's also smart, hardworking, upbeat, and eager to learn. When a major corporate reorganization threatens his department (and everyone in it), Gray decides to step forward and lead the fight for survival. But our hero isn't fully prepared to face his own Milquetoast reputation, skeptical coworkers, political landmines, a scheming rival, and an ugly economy. Can he pull it off and win a promotion? Or will he lose everything and be reduced to nothing more than kingpin of his impressive model railroad? No one cares what happens more than . . .

Taupe Blanderson

Gray's wife, and the telecommuting marketing director for one of the city's new high-tech firms. She juggles a full-time job, household chores, parenthood, volunteer responsibilities, and frequent travel and makes it all look easy. How does she do it? Is it the cottage cheese and root beer pops that fill her office refrigerator? Or is it a set of hard-earned skills she can teach Gray before it's too late? And can she help Gray face the challenge of his life and still find time to teach . . .

Kelly and Violet Blanderson

Gray and Taupe's children. Neither could care less about Gray's struggle. Kelly is too busy pouting about the unfair treatment he receives from his Little League Coach Butthead, plotting to free his classroom's hamsters, and running a black market video game ring. Meanwhile, Violet is desperate to win the approval of the high school's popular kids and the attention of the junior class heartbreaker. It's enough drama for Gray, Taupe and . . .

Mavis Davis

The Blandersons' wise, mysterious, earth mother babysitter. She's an aging hippie who still drives her VW van and marches in protests, but somehow her personal friends have included the Dalai Lama, Princess Di, Walt Disney, Bill Gates, and hundreds of others. She has an uncanny knack for appearing at just the right moment and always knowing exactly what's going on—and what's about to happen. Her advice to Gray is invaluable, including her encouragement to befriend the old soul . . .

Consuelo (Connie) Sanchez

Recent immigrant from Costa Rica who works in the company warehouse. Although not technically the boss, she is a key figure because the others in the department look up to her. She's a great listener and also has great common sense. When Gray seeks her advice about how to cope with change ("Reorganization is change? New country, new language, new life . . . lemme tell you, Gray, that's change."), she becomes a key ally in his struggle. Connie has a soft heart, but she tells it like it is. And no one in the warehouse will forget the day she stopped a coworker's whining by plugging his mouth with a pacifier. She becomes a mentor to Gray's other ally . . .

S. P. Chang

Gen-X information systems expert who sets high standards for herself but often struggles to meet those standards on time. She's found 127 Mr. Rights through online dating, and then missed every date for what she asserts are "very good reasons." Smart, hip, and totally impatient with Global Gadget's "idiot bureaucracy," she can see the bigger picture and comes up with the idea that may just save the day. Of course, it would all be a lot easier if it weren't for . . .

Rick Newman

Hotshot sales star who does great work but never misses a chance to promote himself: He forgot to send flowers to his girlfriend on her birthday, but sent them to the CEO's wife when she finished remodeling her house. When Gray misreads office politics and embarrasses Rick, Rick declares war on Gray's initiative and will stop at nothing to ruin him. Rick is determined to take over the department so that he can fire Gray. But in his angry single-mindedness he carelessly shares information that the company is hiding from the press and he overlooks . . .

Addison Applebaum III

Finance guy who does everything by the book, perfectly, and hates any change or confrontation. But Addison has access to financial records, and after being ridiculed or ignored by the other employees, he eats up Gray's interest in the books and reveals things management would prefer to keep quiet. Addison sorts his trash by color and won't come to the department potluck without warning labels about ingredients that may cause allergic reactions. He couldn't be more different from . . .

Sherman Fox

The laid-back, hard-to-manage creative marketing guy. He came up with an award-winning idea that earned the company lots of money—and he also organized a sick-out when the company tried to remove the soda vending machine. He supports Gray when he's in the mood to, but his support for the turnaround plan is critical. Can S. P. win him over? Her job would be easier if he were as committed and hardworking as . . .

Noreen St. Mary

Lead administrative support employee and the hardest-working, most committed person on the staff—just ask her. Wears her long hours on her sleeve, even if it isn't clear what she does all that time. Uses pencils until she can barely hold them and once went three weeks with a burned-out light bulb in her cubicle because "no one ever promised work would be easy." She wants Gray to succeed, but her world-weary cynicism frequently gets in her way. If only she were as carefree as . . .

Juan Del Toro

Logistics guy who works so he can have a great personal life. Applies himself sporadically, except when it comes to dating. Constantly tests the rules. He wears too much cologne and has the personal online handle DosEquis (XX). He's also deeper than he seems, a closet philosopher and sometime mentor to Gray. His combination of brains and brawn has attracted the interest of . . .

Barbie Falwell

Bright intern who learns quickly and offers good ideas, but still sees the world in simplistic, highly moral terms. She uses floral magnets to keep quotes from Mother Teresa and Oprah on her file drawers. Gray learns to depend on her for the truth, because in her innocence she tells it like it is, without the filter of politics or too many bad experiences. She and all the others ultimately work for . . .

Virginia Edgarly

Gray's boss. Senior Vice President responsible for Gray's division and two other (and more profitable) divisions. Mastermind of the reorganization, she's determined to make it work and become the next CEO. Only a fool would bet against Virginia: She never calls AAA—she changes her own tires. She ultimately must choose between Gray and Rick, and each thinks he has the inside track. Who's right? It may not matter. Virginia is paying more attention to . . .

Rudy "Buzz" Bravado

The division's biggest customer. Whether he keeps buying or bolts for another supplier will decide it all. Only Gray and S. P. seem to realize that, but will their insight be enough to give them the upper hand? It won't be easy: Buzz is demanding, profane, and never, ever wrong. Buzz chews with his mouth open and has never, ever used a salad fork. Let the battle begin. . . .

Part 1

HOW BUSINESS WORKS

chapter one

Change

How to Thrive during Uncertainty by Driving Change

My boss, Virginia—she's the head of our division—is obsessed with Hollywood. She talks about it all the time. I don't mean that she talks about the stars and the Academy Awards and all the stuff you read about in *People* magazine. She talks about The Industry—the business side of making movies. Mostly, she talks about how stupid the people running Hollywood are.

She seems to think that a lot of what they do is stupid, but she reserves a special contempt for what she calls their resistance to change. She says that Hollywood has resisted every single innovation: sound, color, television, home video, digital technology, and now DVDs. Each time, they said that the change would kill the movies and fought against it. Yet each time, not only did the world not end but audiences embraced the change and the result was a lot more profit. She thinks they should have learned by now, but they haven't.

If they haven't learned, Virginia is determined not to make the same mistake. She's very proud of her comfort with change. Personally, I'm not sure she really gets it. She shows off her adaptability by buying every new device that comes along—her briefcase looks like a Sharper Image outlet. She also hasn't met an idea yet that she didn't like. Our finance guy, Addison, keeps all his old memos in binders. I joke with him that he should donate them to the Smithsonian because they document every business trend of the last 15 years: diversity, Total Quality Management, outdoor team building, and on and on. We've lived it all. For 15 minutes.

Don't Mistake Novelty for Change.

I finally decided that Virginia just got bored too easily. She packaged her short attention span as a virtue. It might have been a pretty entertaining personality quirk except that it affected all of us. Once Virginia gave us an article by Peter Drucker to read. He said something in it that really caught our attention: "So much of what we call management consists in making it difficult for people to work." That's sure how all of Virginia's new ideas struck us.

If you want evidence that they weren't all important, here it is: Nothing changed. Virginia created a veneer of change, but that's all it was. She presented every change—whether new rules for recording a voice mail greeting or a whole new business model—exactly the same way. Each one was announced with great fanfare (usually in a long meeting that took us away from real work) and included some cursory training. Then we never heard about it again.

Real, Sustained Change Happens in Context.

Most of Virginia's programs never had a chance because she was so easily bored. But there was another problem, too: They weren't anchored to anything; they were just trendy.

All that changed when Virginia announced that management was reorganizing Global Gadget. It was the first time that change was really necessary. As you'll see, trying to change has been a series of ups and downs. In the process I've learned that real change only happens when it either solves a problem or exploits an opportunity.

Think about the people around you who change their behavior. You'll find that they do it because an ongoing problem becomes an imminent threat (my wife Taupe stopped smoking when she got pregnant, for example) or because they can expect a real improvement in their lives (as when my colleague Connie Sanchez moved to the United States).

One reason the change we've been through has been so powerful is that it solved a problem *and* helped us exploit an opportunity.

Sustained, Effective Change Demands Sustained, Focused Effort.

Of course, even when there are good reasons to change, it isn't easy. Change requires focus and effort. Even with our survival at stake, it took several months for our change effort just to gain traction and momentum. In today's world, advertisers are creating 15-second commercials because they are afraid that 30-second versions tax people's patience. In this climate, you can imagine how difficult it is to sustain something for months. But it has to be done, so one of the burdens on anyone managing change is to keep the effort fresh.

Another burden is to engage people. A lot of "experts" will tell you that people resist change. I don't think that's true. Think about your home. Suppose some guy came to your house and forced you to change the paint color, hang new art, and replace your furniture with something he chose for you. You would resist, right? But now suppose that the same person hands you a check and invites you to buy art or furniture that *you* choose. Are you as likely to resist?

People Don't Resist Change. They Resist Loss of Control.

Even though it's difficult, people will embrace change if they understand the reason for it and can help shape the outcome. It took time, but ultimately our whole team was 100 percent behind our effort. We've proven that change may be inevitable, but it isn't inevitably painful.

Memo

To: All Associates, Appliances Division
From: Virginia Edgarly
CC: M. Wellington Wadsworth, CEO
Date: 3/10/01
Re: New Business Opportunities

As you are aware, a mandatory meeting of all Appliance Division associates is scheduled for 3:00 p.m. tomorrow in the Learning Center. In advance of the meeting, I wanted to outline some of what I will be announcing. Until tomorrow's announcement, this information is still subject to change.

Global Gadget has a proud history as the world's top supplier of high-quality gadgets. Our product innovations have transformed the industry even as our earnings have defied Wall Street's expectations and paid a strong dividend to our shareholders. That said, in today's fast-paced world no company can rest on its laurels. That includes Global Gadget, which is why we are pursuing a new strategy to improve our market share in key product categories.

You'll see many changes in the coming weeks. The primary focus of our energy, however, will be creating a new division. To date, you all know that the Appliance Division has supplied gadgets to the makers of both large appliances (such as refrigerators and washing machines) and small appliances (such as blenders and hair dryers). Moving forward, the existing Appliance Division will be renamed the Small Appliance Division and will supply only customers in that market.

The new Large Appliance Division will assume our existing business in this market and will be asked to generate more business. This new division will be staffed primarily by associates to be reassigned from other divisions to be determined. For now, I will head both divisions.

Clearly, this change cannot happen overnight. Together, we must create new A to Z processes that will stick. We must coherently pursue synergies that will allow for effective deployment of resources and help us maximize opportunities. In many cases, we must do more with less. And we must embrace change as a positive force.

At this time, we do not plan to rightsize or otherwise change the status of our associates. We will revisit the success of this initiative in six months.

I know that you have many questions. You can ask them in tomorrow's meeting. Beyond that, information will continue to cascade to you. I look forward to working with you through this exciting transition, and I know that I can count on your support.

Figure 1.1 *This is the memo that started everything. As it turned out, she wasn't telling us everything.*

food for thought

Gray's Notebook

1. *Are you clinging to the status quo? Identify three incidents during the past week in which someone asked you to do something different (e.g., changed a regularly scheduled meeting, changed a procedure, changed a project deadline). How did you respond to the change? If you resisted, think about why. Was the change more time consuming for you? Was it less convenient? Or was it just different?*
2. *What's your track record? How can you be seen as more reliable?*
3. *Indy 500 pit crews taught Southwest Airlines how to turn planes around faster. Who can teach you? Identify one thing that your company or department needs to be better at. What expertise is involved? Who has that expertise? Look outside the organization.*
4. *The corporate immune system always resists change. Do you have the stuff to fight the good fight? Think about change you have initiated or plan to initiate. Do you believe in the change enough to fight for it? Identify people or situations that have the potential to thwart your initiative. Do you have a plan to overcome the setbacks?*

Addison's Brain Trust

Wait, there's more! Check out these books for additional information and insight:

> *The Goal* by Eliyahu Goldratt (North River Press, 1992)
> *Harvard Business Review on Change* (Harvard Business School Press, 1998)

S.P. Surfs the Internet

Which movie title best describes change in your organization?

- ★ *The Big Easy* (we like change): 14.2%
- ★ *The Big Sleep* (we don't change): 38.7%
- ★ *The Big Blue* (we don't like change): 46.9%

Source: WorkingWounded.com/ABCnews.com online ballot

Rick's Smart Talk

"If you don't like change, you're going to like irrelevance a lot less."

—*Gen. Eric K. Shinseki*

Connie's Smart Questions

When Virginia announced the reorganization, everyone in our division started complaining that *everything* would change. That was just silly. I moved from Costa Rica, and even then *everything* didn't change. I still eat mangos and I still wash my hair, you know? Some things change, others don't. What's important is to figure out how much what does change matters to you. Think about what matters most to you in your job and ask yourself these questions:

- What is changing?
- Why is it changing?
- What will stay the same?
- Will the change mean that I'll have to work harder?
- What about the change will make my life easier?
- What about the change will make my life harder?
- How will *I* have to change to adapt to this change?
- What can we learn from this change to make it easier next time?
- What will happen to our organization if we don't make this change?

Now ask yourself one final question: Can you live with the change? If not, then you have to make a different change to find what you need.

Gray's Anatomy of Business

I think Taupe almost divorced me when we were buying our house. It was a huge step, and another couple was also bidding on the place. The other couple made an offer that was right at the top of what we could afford, and I didn't know whether to top their offer or to withdraw. That really meant that I couldn't decide whether to make a change. Taupe, the real estate agent, and the owners all wanted an answer. Finally, Mavis took me aside one evening. She told me that there was risk in acting (in making the change), but there was also risk in *not* acting (leaving things as they were). She made me see that there were consequences of both decisions, not just the one to make the offer.

Then she gave me a tool that was really helpful. I've used it ever since. You might find it helpful, too. First, think of something that you've been sitting on the fence about. Then make two lists. (The lists in the example are very short, but you should make your list as long as it needs to be.) On the left side, list the benefits of moving forward. When we bought the house, for example, I wrote down having more room, enrolling the kids in better schools, and a shorter commute time. For each benefit, assign a score from 1 to 5. If the benefit is really important to you, give it a 5; if it's not very important, give it a 1. For the house, the better schools were a 5 but the built-in workbench in the garage was a 1. Then, on the right side, list the benefits of leaving things as they are. Assign points in the same way. Now add up the positive and negative scores. Place them on the teeter-totter below. Which side has the higher number? The heavier side of the teeter-totter shows you which argument is stronger.

_____	_____
_____	_____
_____	_____
TOTAL	_____

Barbie's Brainy Glossary

Change   To make different in some particular or radical way. Like when I told Ben to get lost after I found him kissing that other girl.

Irrelevant   Not having significant impact on the issue at hand. Like when Mother tells me Ben would still be my boyfriend if I wore different makeup.

Reorganization   The financial reconstruction of a business concern; organizing things differently. Like when the nice man at the bank showed me how to transfer all my credit card bills to a new credit card so I could write just 1 check instead of 14.

Status Quo   How things already are.

chapter two

Walk Your Talk

How to Earn Respect by Aligning What You Say with What You Do

Before Global Gadget's reorganization, I went to work every day and lied. I'm not talking about the kind of whoppers that would have been really obvious to anyone. In fact, if you had accused me of lying I would have been shocked. I prided myself on being frank and sincere. But now, in hindsight, I can see the fibs plain as day. Here's how they would happen:

We had regular team meetings to discuss the status of projects. As a group, we committed to a schedule or deadline. At the end of every meeting, whoever was in charge would ask whether everyone was on board and I always nodded. I believed I *was* on board. But then I would begin to work on my product designs and I would find a problem in the design, or find something else that would stand in the way of my deadline. Each time I would take the time to fix the problem. After all, we didn't just want it done, we wanted it done right, didn't we?

I completed the drawings, confident that they were right, and felt really good about my contribution. But other people weren't seeing me as such a team player. My drawings were always late, and everyone else had to scramble to do their part to meet the deadline. That meant that they ended up working late or coming in on the weekend. Some of them thought I didn't care about them or about their jobs—only about myself. Others thought I just couldn't do my job very well because I could never seem to meet deadlines.

I wasn't walking my talk. The way the others saw it, I said one thing ("I'm a team player") and then did things that suggested my work was more important than everyone else's.

Don't Make Commitments You Aren't Sure You Can Keep. If You Can't Meet a Commitment, Think About and Deal with the Effects.

For a long time I was able to coast along despite my behavior. After all, nothing I did was so terrible that we ever missed an important deadline or lost a contract. What did it really matter if I was late if it also meant the work was better? Well, it mattered because all along I was developing a reputation—and not a good one—that would come back to bite me. I learned that actions really do speak louder than words.

I shouldn't have been surprised. I form my opinions of others based on their actions—and you probably do, too. Let's say your boss says that a work-life balance is important, that everyone needs time with his or her family or to pursue interests outside the office. She encourages you to take vacations, stay out of the office on weekends, and leave early once in a while to attend your kid's soccer game or school play. Now, let's say that this same boss comes to work early and usually works late. She hasn't taken a vacation in three years, and when she did go away she called in every day. You've never known her to leave early even to go to the doctor, let alone plan to do something with her kids. So what's the "truth"? Does she value work-family balance or not?

If you took that boss at her word and rarely worked late and sometimes left early to go to a soccer game, then you are a stronger person than I am. Most people follow the example set by the boss, because they believe that if they don't, they will be passed over for a promotion, or miss out on the cool assignments, or be the first to go if there's a downturn.

We All Predict What Other People Will Do and What They Can Produce Based on What We've Seen Them Do Before.

You could argue that it doesn't really matter if the boss says one thing and does another. She's the boss and can do what she wants. Since everyone knows she doesn't really mean it when she talks about leaving on time, it all works out. But the reality is that it doesn't.

For one thing, no one really listens because we're all a bit skeptical. Instead, everyone waits to see what the boss will do. Imagine that she says she wants new ideas. Will the staff offer their ideas? No. Most people will wait to see how she reacts to the first new idea. If she dismisses it, ridicules it, or ignores it, that will be the last idea she gets. Not only will some potentially great ideas be lost, but the staff will lose a lot of time waiting and watching and talking to each other about what the boss *really* wants. In short, she's lost their trust and that shows up in many ways. If she says there's a crisis, then people will wait to see if she acts like there's a crisis. If she promises a raise, people will be skeptical. And some people—the ones who accepted a job believing they would have work-family balance and really want that—will leave.

If a Boss Is Inconsistent in What He or She Says or Does about One Issue, Most Employees Won't Trust What He or She Says about Anything.

I learned all that after Virginia announced the reorganization. I saw that most people on our team didn't really see the urgency of the situation—they didn't trust Virginia. I understand why they felt that way, because she had said one thing and done another before. But the reorganization was real, and I knew that the finances weren't going to be in our favor unless we all worked together and did something—and fast.

I decided to try and get people moving. As you'll see, that was easier said than done. No one really trusted me either, not back then. And why should they? All they saw was a guy who didn't make waves and then missed his deadlines.

First you have to stand for something. Then you have to walk your talk.

Perfect. Now Virginia thinks I'm a loser.
Hellooooo
I brought you a nice lemonade because life is giving you lemons.
Thanks, Barbie
You know, I had a great idea – And nobody got it.
Oh Gray, Don't be blue. Hee Hee
Leaders are born, not made. And, well, you know we all like you, right?
more lemonade?

food for thought

Gray's Notebook

1. Do you really watch and listen to what you do and say at work? Try consciously being aware at your next meeting. Write down your thoughts.
2. List three of your most dearly held values. How do they influence your action at work? For each value, list two ways in which you expressed that value within the last month. For example, if you value honesty, write down two ways in which you were honest. Ask yourself whether there were any situations at work in which you did not respect your values—in which, for example, you were not honest. Why did you ignore your own values in those situations? What can you do differently next time?
3. Do your actions support your values? Ask two coworkers you respect and trust. What did they say?
4. Develop a personal plan to better align your walk and talk. Identify a way in which your walk and talk are out of sync. List three ways in which you could be more consistent in what you say and do; commit to taking those actions over the next two weeks. Make a note to yourself every time you do it. At the end of the two weeks, choose another way in which your walk and talk are out of sync and follow the same steps. Once a month, make a point of asking someone you trust whether they have noticed a difference.

Addison's Brain Trust

Wait, there's more! Check out these books for additional information and insight:

Walk Your Talk by Kare Anderson (Ten Speed, 1994)
The Boss's Survival Guide by Bob Rosner, Allan Halcrow, and Alan Levins (McGraw-Hill, 2001)

S.P. Surfs for the Internet

In a survey conducted by Manchester, Inc., people were asked what their coworkers do that most undermines trust. Here's what they said:

- ★ Act inconsistently in what say and do: 69%
- ★ Seek personal gain above shared gain: 41%
- ★ Withhold information: 34%
- ★ Lie or tell half-truths: 33%

Rick's Smart Talk

"It's not what you don't know that hurts you, it's what you think that just ain't so."—
Satchel Paige

Connie's Smart Questions

When you attend meetings, pay attention to how you participate:

- Do you share information, or do you withhold it?
- When do you speak up? When you agree, when you don't agree, or both?
- Do you say that you agree even if you don't?
- Do you share an opinion only after someone else has expressed the same opinion?
- What do you do if someone challenges something you've said? Do you defend or explain your point of view, or do you retreat?
- Do you commit to deadlines that you know are unrealistic?
- Do you express one opinion before a meeting and then express a different one during it?
- If someone reminds you of something you said earlier, do you deny that you said it?

Keep "minutes" of your meeting behavior. Pay attention to how often you express how you really feel. You'll earn respect if you say what you think almost all the time.

Gray's Anatomy of Business

My Big Fat Greek Wedding kept me awake night after night. It wasn't because the father in the movie reminded me of my father-in-law (though I do hide our cleaning supplies when he visits). It was because once when I was traveling on company business I watched the movie on one of those pay channels. I left the charge on my hotel bill when I turned in my expenses, even though I knew we weren't supposed to. It just ate at me until I couldn't take it anymore—I confessed everything to Addison and paid for the movie. Inside, I just couldn't be dishonest, you know? Think about what you just couldn't do (or, if you'd rather, what you have to do). When you run up against a feeling inside that just won't budge, that's a value. List three of your values. Think about the ones that come up at work, not "no sex until the third date" or something like that:

1. _____
2. _____
3. _____

Do you pay attention to how you express your values at work? I didn't; I was too busy doing stuff to even think about it. But even if you haven't been paying attention, other people have. We all observe one another at work, and we draw conclusions based on what we see. I mean, I could tell on her first day that S.P. values honesty because she told Addison right to his face that he was too uptight. I was impressed that she told him instead of just telling the rest of us. Think about someone you work with that you respect.

List three of that person's values; beside each one, write something that person has said or done that expresses that value.

1. _____
2. _____
3. _____

Barbie's Glossary

Cost/benefit ratio   A financial analysis that determines a numerical value for the cost effectiveness of an activity or purchase. Like when I'm in the store and I really want to buy the cute shoes, and I have to figure out how many outfits I can wear them with to know whether they're worth the price.

Potluck   An event when everyone in the office (except for the people who think they are too busy or too good to do it) makes some food and brings it to work to show everyone else how good a cook they are. Sometimes we talk about work.

Values   What we believe in such an essential, deep-seated way that it drives how we behave and the choices we make. Like how I could never shoplift anything, even if Winona Ryder does it.

Walk the Talk   When what someone says and what he or she does convey the same message. Like when someone says, "I'm trying to lose weight," and then at lunch they order a salad instead of the lasagna.

The Zone   A state of mind reached by creative people when ideas flow, things turn out the way they hoped they would, and they no longer want to put their head in the oven. The artist's version of a good hair day.

chapter three

Dollars and Sense

How to Use Your Company's Financial Data to Set Priorities

Can you name your company's top-selling product or service? Can you name your company's most profitable product or service? Do you know which three customers buy most from your company and what they buy? Do you know where your company forecasts financial growth and where management sees a decline? Until recently, I had no idea. I should have—and so should you.

Most of the time, I looked at my pay stub to be sure that my check was correct. Sometimes, I didn't even do that. What a mistake! I should have looked at *every* pay stub—and that's just the beginning. I also should have followed the company's stock price, read the annual report, and paid close attention to my department's budget.

Unless You Really Understand Your Company's Finances, You Are Working in the Dark.

I found a lot of reasons not to pay attention to the money stuff. We have a whole finance department, and I thought it was their job to deal with financial issues. I thought that if the company really wanted me to know something about the finances my boss would tell me. Also, I hate to balance my checkbook and pay bills, so learning about company finance just seemed too hard. I said before that those are reasons not to learn about finances, but they aren't really reasons—they're excuses.

Yes, your company must have a finance department (or at least an accountant). It's that department's or person's job to know and manage the detail, but that doesn't let you off the hook. Turn the situation around and look at it from the other side: Would it be all right if your financial people had no knowledge of the rest of your business? Suppose you work for a rental car company. Could the finance department be effective without knowing which cars the company rents, how long people rent them, or what extra services (such as insurance) people buy? Of course not.

If you're like most people, your boss probably doesn't sit down and give you regular financial updates. (My boss, Virginia, never shared financial information at meetings.) That doesn't mean your boss doesn't think you need to know. Your boss has a lot of other things to focus on. Financial data is available. Information is in an annual report, online, or even in the newspaper. If investors in your company think this information is important, shouldn't you?

(If you work for a small, privately held company, financial information is private. The owner may not want to share specifics, such as how much profit the company made. Even so, you can probably get the answers to the questions I posed at the beginning of this section. Ask!)

I won't kid you that finance is easy. It can be complex and confusing, especially in large companies. Technology can be complicated, too. Some software is hard to learn, but you can't tell your boss that it's too hard and just opt out. You have to learn what you need to know to do your job. But while you may need to know how to create a spreadsheet, you don't have to be able to write a spreadsheet program. It's the same with finance: You need to understand it, but you don't need to be an expert.

Don't Wait to Be Told. It's Your Job to Get the Financial Information You Need.

Once you have the information, you can be much more effective. That may surprise you; it surprised me. I ran smack into that reality, though, as soon as we started to plan how we were going to turn our division around.

Rick argued that he would just sell more. That sounds so logical: Sell more product, bring in more revenue, problem solved. It turns out to be faulty logic, at least in this case. We completely forgot to consider our expenses. Oops. We also overlooked the balance between revenue and expenses, and the process of fulfilling orders. In short, we only looked at part of the equation.

S.P. gave me an example that made it easier to understand, so I thought I would share it with you, too. Imagine you run a hotel and your goal is to make more money. You could decide to add more rooms to the hotel. If you have more rooms, you can make more money—right? Only if those rooms are full, or at least enough of them are full that the revenue covers expenses. If too few people book those new rooms, then you'll actually lose money.

In the hotel business, the key indicator of financial health is the occupancy rate, and you can see why. We faced a similar challenge in our business, but until the reorganization only Addison saw that. If we hadn't stopped to really consider the financial issues, we would have spent all our energy pursuing the wrong goal. Think of the time we would have wasted and the useless work we would have done! Worse, we would have failed. Getting our heads around the financial issues was key to everything else we did.

Know Your Company's Key Financial Indicators, and Use That Knowledge to Set Priorities and Focus Your Energy.

You know that nothing in business is that simple. Just knowing our key financial indicators all by themselves was not enough—we still had to figure out how to improve our performance. At least we were starting down the right path, and we had learned a crucial lesson: Everything about the company's dollars must make sense.

food for thought

Gray's Notebook

1. *Avoid MEGO (my eyes glaze over). Don't picture numbers in your mind. Instead, think in terms of what you actually produce or the service you provide. For example, translate your break-even point to a specific number of sofas made, wine bottles shipped, room nights sold, or whatever's appropriate to your business. Then think in terms of how much profit the company makes for all business beyond that. Then you can think in terms of action: "This week, we need to do eight more haircuts."*

2. *What is your company's critical number? (Hint: In a hotel it is occupancy rate.) If you don't know, review your company's annual report or earnings statements. If you work for a privately held company, ask someone in the finance department for help.*

3. *What is your department or division's critical number? How does your department support the company's overall critical number? (For example, if you work in food service at a hotel, you can't directly affect occupancy rate. However, occupancy rate is important because it drives revenue. You can drive revenue by upselling room service orders or offering superior service so that guests are inclined to use room service again.) What can you do personally to improve your department's critical number?*

4. *How can you help the bottom line by wasting less or cutting costs? List three ways you can save money. Offer the suggestions to your boss.*

5. *Have you ever had an idea for another product or service that your company could offer to generate more revenue? Explore what would be involved in making it happen.*

Addison's Brain Trust

Wait, there's more! Check out these books for additional information and insight:

The Great Game of Business by Jack Stack (Currency, 1992)
The Open Book Experience by John Case (Perseus, 1998)

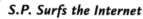

S.P. Surfs the Internet

Which movie sums up your company's future prospects?

- ★ *Apocalypse Now:* 44.7%
- ★ *Ordinary People:* 30%
- ★ *Fantastic Voyage:* 25.2%

Source: WorkingWounded.com/ABCnews.com online ballot

Rick's Smart Talk

"Dollars do better if they are accompanied by sense."

—*Earl Riney*

Connie's Smart Questions

Money at my house is a simple thing. I tell you, there's one key indicator I look at, honey: Did more money come in this month than is going out? I know how much we have to bring in to meet our fixed expenses, like the mortgage. But I also work to bring in more, because something else is going to happen—the washer will break, the kids will need something for school, whatever. I also look at something Addison tells me are ratios. I look at my credit card statement to see how much we owe versus our limit. I like to know how much room we have if we need it. That's it. You know, the money in business isn't so much different. It's just bigger—much bigger. Ask yourself these questions:

- What are your major goals at work?
- How will you know if you've achieved your goals?
- How do you measure progress toward your goals?
- Stuck? Whenever I get stuck, I look at ratios. For example, if I worked in a restaurant I'd look at the ratio of tables to the number of customers. (How many tables are full? How often?) What ratios would give you valuable information?
- Once you've determined some key ratios, benchmark how you're doing compared to other businesses (libraries have books full of ratios, just so you can see how you're doing).
- Focus on a few key ratios that have the greatest impact on your business. Which ones are key? Why?

Make a chart of your company's key indicators and ratios. Post it in your work space, and look at it every day. Think about what you're doing to support those numbers.

Gray's Anatomy of Business

Play chief financial officer (CFO) for a day. Develop three ways you can either increase revenue or decrease costs. Be sure to make them as practical as possible. Once you've come up with your list, talk to the key players who would need to be involved in implementing your ideas. Ask for their feedback to improve on your original ideas.

Barbie's Brainy Glossary

Bottom line   The last line of a financial report that shows net profit or loss. Everyone around here uses this to mean "the end result." Why don't they just say that?

Cash flow   A measure of a company's liquidity. How much cash comes in (versus what is billed) so that it is available to meet expenses.

Just-in-Time   A philosophy of manufacturing based on planned elimination of all waste and continuous improvement of productivity. It's also about meeting customer needs as they arise.

Liquidity   Cash or goods capable of being easily converted to cash. Like in high school when Mandy went to that pawn shop in the awful part of town to get cash to get the car fixed before her parents got back from vacation.

Profit   Excess of returns over expenditures. What's left over after the bills are paid.

Tofurkey   Faux meat made from tofu and shaped to look like turkey. S.P. says it helps her stay slim, but personally I'd rather do an aerobics class.

chapter four

Politics

How to Maneuver through Workplace Dynamics—
Good and Bad—to Get Things Done

Taupe and I always host the family Thanksgiving gathering at our place. I judge the day a success if the turkey is edible (we don't talk about the year that Kelly added his dirty socks to the dressing after the turkey was in the oven) and none of the guests leave in tears. In other words, I judge the food and the politics.

Until Global Gadget's reorganization, I thought politics was something that happened in Washington. But then I really messed up, and I learned that politics happens at work, too.

Consider this situation: An employee learns that his division is in financial trouble. Unwilling to let the division collapse, he decides something has to be done. He organizes a meeting of the entire division. At the meeting, the group comes up with a plan for change. Employees take responsibility for parts of the plan and begin to implement it. But the employee never mentions any of this to his boss, the division head. Pretty stupid, isn't it? But that's what I did. The story is about me.

You've probably seen similar political blunders in your workplace: failing to listen, surprising people, burning bridges, being inconsistent, or choosing the wrong timing. Those are only a few of the political mistakes we can make. What they all have in common is a disregard for other people. These mistakes happen when we ignore how our actions affect other people.

Everything We Do at Work Affects Other People.

Once we've stepped on someone's toes, the political fallout is easy to see. People get angry and lash out. They draw lines in the sand and work hard to get even. They get hurt feelings and sulk. They withdraw. More often than not, they assume the worst. It's funny, isn't it, that people judge themselves on their intentions and judge others on their actions?

In one sense, it's easy to dismiss this sort of workplace politics as childish emotions. There are days when I really think a sandbox referee would do us a lot of good. Although dismissing politics is tempting, it would also be a mistake. Beneath the emotions are some real workplace issues that keep us from doing our best work or meeting our goals.

My mistake in leaving Virginia out of the loop is a good example. Suppose that her boss (the CEO) heard about our plan and went to Virginia with a criticism or even a question. Because she didn't know anything, Virginia would be embarrassed. The CEO might conclude that Virginia didn't know what was happening in her own division. I defy you to find a good spin on putting your boss in an awkward situation.

With your boss out of the loop, your project doesn't benefit either. For one thing, there's no chance for you to learn from your boss's experience or insight. Beyond that, you miss out on key support. A good boss works to clear paths for you as you work, removing obstacles and getting you the tools you need. But a boss can't clear a path she doesn't even know about.

(You may be thinking that your boss doesn't clear paths for you, or that he or she is more likely to say "no" than "yes." If you ask, you may be surprised. But even if the answer is "no," wouldn't you rather hear that now than after you've invested a lot in the idea?)

I didn't think of any of that when I charged ahead without talking to Virginia. I didn't stop to think about how she could help (or even what help I might need), or about how our plans might affect her. That wasn't the only political mistake I made, either. You'll see that there were other times I didn't consider other people and didn't tell the whole truth when I could have. Every mistake cost me time and undercut our progress. I guess I'm a slow learner.

Being Political Isn't about Being Nice or Kissing Up. It's about Getting Work Done Effectively.

There are times when politics is the hardest work of all. It took me time, but eventually I saw that I had made mistakes and I fixed them. Some people never see their political gaffes; others see them but refuse to own them or change their behavior. They either won't or can't do things differently, and they are a pain to work with. I'm sure you've worked with one or two of them.

You can't change those people. What you can do is become an expert politician and work around them. That's what I call *positive politics*. Maybe that sounds crazy to you. Once at a neighborhood barbecue I asked people about the politics at work. Every single example that people came up with was negative. People complained a lot about the politics at work, and how much they disliked it. But after we talked about it a while, people began to admit that maybe politics doesn't have to be negative.

Has anyone at work done you a favor recently? Lent you a pen, brought lunch back for you, covered a meeting for you, anything? If you're like me, you get so caught up in negativity that you don't notice when people help you. Or you notice that people are helping, but you take it for granted.

Politics Isn't Always Negative. There's Greater Power in Positive Politics.

Actually, positive politics takes effort. It requires staying focused on the big picture and then doing what we can to help everyone get to the goal. Think about professional football teams. The players make a lot more money than you or I do, but they are employees. Their goal is to win the game, and to do that they help each other. They pass the ball, they block the tackle, or whatever's required. That's positive politics. (If you doubt that it's politics, imagine the reaction if a quarterback refused to move the ball. See what I mean?) But none of it happens without practice—lots of practice.

We can practice positive politics, too. We can practice listening, preparing people, building bridges, being consistent, and carefully choosing our timing. If I had been smart enough to have seen that clearly, I never would have gotten into trouble with Rick. But when I made my mistakes, somehow I knew to build relationships with S.P. and Connie and to build for the future.

Negative politics is a waste of time. Practice positive politics and see what you can achieve.

PROJECT REPORT CARD

GLOBAL GADGET

I. POLITICS

       GRADE _____

LISTENING (*Assign one point for each criterion met*)
- Sought input of all stakeholders
- Incorporated suggestions, or explained reasons for not doing so
- Accepted feedback profitably

EXPLAINING (*Assign one point for each criterion met*)
- Offered the rationale for all decisions
- Provided data/evidence to support rationale
- Advocated for the project within the organization

SUPPORTING (*Assign one point for each criterion met*)
- Was a team player (e.g., supported others, shared credit, promoted cooperation)
- Acknowledged the contributions of others
- Continued to support other projects

TIMING (*Assign one point for each criterion met*)
- Allowed adequate time to complete the project within a reasonable time frame
- Identified project milestones and adjusted timeline as needed
- Timed project not to overlap with/interfere with other projects

BRIDGE BUILDING (*Assign one point for each criterion met*)
- Took responsibility for errors or problems; offered solutions
- Told the truth
- Looked to learn—not blame—when problems arose

CONSISTENCY (*Assign one point for each criterion met*)
- Reported the same information to all parties
- Walked the talk
- Saw the project through to conclusion

WORKING WITH ALLIES (*Assign one point for each criterion met*)
- Identified at least one ally to support the project
- Reviewed project specifics with the ally
- Relied on the ally for support and feedback throughout

II. PROJECT QUALITY

     GRADE _____

DEFECTS/ERRORS (*Assign one point for each criterion met*)
- Established quality standards and monitored quality
- Corrected defects/errors (or problem that resulted in errors)
- Met or exceeded quality standards

DEADLINE (*Assign one point for each criterion met*)
- Developed adequate timeline for the project
- Monitored progress toward goal and adjusted timeline as needed
- Completed project on time or early

BUDGET (*Assign one point for each criterion met*)
- Developed budget or anticipated costs
- Monitored expenses and adjusted budget as needed
- Met or beat budget

PROCEDURES (*Assign one point for each criterion met*)
- Defined project process/procedures
- Communicated process/procedures to all involved
- Monitored adherence to procedures and adjusted procedures as needed

GOALS (*Assign one point for each criterion met*)
- Defined project goals
- Communicated goals to all stakeholders
- Met or exceeded project goals

To compute grades: For each category, add the number of points assigned (maximum of 3 possible in each category). 0 or 1 = F; 2 = C; 3 = A

Figure 4.1 *Sherman's observation that all work gets two grades—one for quality and one for politics—really stuck with me. I found myself spending a lot of time thinking about the grades I was earning. Finally, I decided to really figure it out and use my grades to help me improve. I developed this form for myself initially, but other people started using it, too.*

food for thought

Gray's Notebook

1. Work always gets two grades: one for quality and one for politics. Think about your most recent project. Which grade would you give it for quality? For politics? Why?
2. Do favors long before you need anything in return.
3. Connect with people in other departments. Find out what they do. Brainstorm ways in which you could work together to help the company.
4. Pay someone else a compliment. Send a thank-you note or e-mail when someone does something nice for you. Tell your boss about something great that someone else did.
5. Play positive politics: Build community, cover someone else's back, lend a hand, volunteer for the task no one else wants to do. Do at least three positive things each week. Make a point of being nice to people who aren't easy to get along with.

Addison's Brain Trust

Wait, there's more! Check out these books for additional information and insight:

Getting Things Done When You're Not in Charge by Geoffrey Bellman (Fireside, 1993)
Positive Politics at Work by Douglas McKenna (McGraw Hill, 1993)

S.P. Surfs the Internet

If you had to describe your company as a TV show, which type would you choose?

* ★ Science fiction: 7%
* ★ Courtroom drama: 10%
* ★ Medical emergency: 18%
* ★ Soap opera: 27%
* ★ Survivor: 38%

Source: New York University Management Institute survey

Rick's Smart Talk

"A company is stronger if it's bound by love than bound by fear."
—*Herb Kelleher, Former CEO of Southwest Airlines*

Connie's Smart Questions

Death, taxes, and politics. Yep, those are the three things we all have to deal with. Let me tell you, you can leave your country and you still have to deal with politics. So if we have to deal with it, it makes sense to be smart about it. Ask yourself these questions:

- Do you accept the role that politics plays at work?
- Who are the effective politicians at work?
- What makes them effective?
- What will you do, and won't you do, at work?
- Look at people who are opposed to what you want to do. Do some digging to see where your interests and theirs overlap. Work from common ground.
- Do you take the time to find out why people take the positions that they take at work?
- What politics do you play at work?

We think of politics as something that happens to us. But think about it this way: If you left your job tomorrow, what politics would you take with you?

Gray's Anatomy of Business

Come up with a list of the three most important changes that have been successfully implemented in your organization over the last five years. Don't just rely on your judgment; talk to other people in your company to see what they think. They can be sexy, splashy public efforts or quiet backroom changes. Now start digging to find out who were the key drivers behind these changes. Talk to them to get the behind-the-scenes view of what really happened. Ask why they decided to make the change. Also ask: What was the biggest obstacle they faced? What was the key to their success? What role did politics play in the process? What did they learn from the process? If they had it to do over again, what would they do differently?

Barbie's Brainy Glossary

Agenda   A plan of things to be done. Around here, though, everyone uses it to mean what someone really wants to get done but isn't saying they really want to get done. Like when you tell your date you'll meet him somewhere because it will be easier when what you really mean is that you don't want him to meet your parents.

Brown-noser   Someone who says only what the boss wants to hear or offers insincere compliments in the interest of staying in favor. Like when Rick tells Virginia she looks nice. Oh, please.

Building bridges   When you do nice things, or listen, or whatever so that you make connections with people.

Politics   Relations between people at work. Not dating or anything, but how we all do or don't get along and what we do or don't do to get along better.

chapter five

Customers

How to Identify What Your Customers Really Think

One Friday night, Taupe and I took the kids to a Mexican restaurant near us. We enjoyed the atmosphere, and we were thrilled to find that the kids would eat a meal that didn't come in a paper sack. Soon we were going every Friday night. It became a ritual to decompress and plan our weekends over tacos. Then on the way home one night Taupe announced that she didn't want to go there again. "No matter how often we go, the owners act as if they've never seen us before," she said. "I just don't feel they value our business." We never went back. These days, we go to a pasta place where the owners greet us warmly and save us a table.

I should have remembered that lesson when we were trying to figure out how to rescue the division. Instead, I did what too many businesses do: I forgot all about the customers. If Virginia hadn't given us a not-so-gentle prod, we might have spent all our time pursuing something the customers didn't care about at all. Today, we'd be unemployed.

Customers May Not Always Be Right, But They Are the Reason We're in Business.

In my defense, unlike the restaurant owner, I never saw our customers. That's a common problem, too. Many employees never see customers, so they don't seem real or important. It happens because although most businesses say they value their customers, they aren't walking their talk.

In some cases, they limp their talk: They encourage good customer service and even provide training to help achieve it, but it stops there. There are no tangible (or even intangible) rewards for exceeding customer expectations. Employees who otherwise wouldn't interact with customers aren't encouraged to do so. The company doesn't identify key customers for employees or share any information about them. It's benign neglect, but neglect all the same.

At least neglect beats hostility. I'm sure you've met flight attendants or retail clerks who made it clear that helping you was interfering with their *real* jobs. Don't blame the employees. When my daughter Violet got a job at a fast food restaurant, the manager told her that closing on time was the top priority. Can you imagine? Making it impossible to accept customer money was the top priority.

Genuinely Valuing Customers Transcends Good Customer Service.

You can't walk in someone else's shoes until you know whether he or she is wearing lumberjack boots, sneakers, or Bruno Magli dress shoes. Given what we've accomplished since Virginia announced the reorganization, I'm embarrassed to admit that when we began none of us could name a single customer. That's especially ironic because of all that we learned from our customers as we worked.

We weren't surprised to learn so much about our customers once we did walk in their shoes. We learned how they use our products, what their business challenges are, and what their competitors are doing. We also learned what other products they're using and why. We learned what keeps them awake at night, and how we can help.

What did surprise us is how much we learned about us. We found out how we were perceived in the market and what our customers didn't like about us. We even discovered some business opportunities that we might never have found on our own.

Customers Are a Source of Information as Much as a Source of Revenue.

The more we learned, the more effective we became. That shouldn't have been a surprise either. We were all used to sharing information with each other and using that information to do our jobs better. Why did we think that sharing information should stop at the front door? Once we started talking with our customers, we found that we could do better not only *for* them, but also *with* them. We opened the door to some partnerships that made good business sense for both companies.

I realize now that we'll never know enough about our customers. But we've come a long way. We know who they are when they come in—and we always have a table waiting.

April 6, 2001

Mr. Rudy "Buzz" Bravado
President
SureSux, Inc.
8801 N. 17th Ave.
Central City, USA 33333

Dear Mr. Bravado:

Thank you for yesterday's telephone call. You have every right to be disappointed that we fell short of our customer service standards. We share your disappointment, but rest assured we will make things right. Your candor is invaluable.

To recap: On April 4 you received an incorrect shipment from Global Gadget. Instead of our gadget #45318 (retractor doohickey), you received a different part. It was not possible for you to use the incorrect part, which delayed production and shipment of product to your customers. We sincerely regret the error.

You no doubt have three questions: (1) What happened? (2) What is Global Gadget going to do about it? (3) How can you trust that this will not happen again?

What happened is that in our warehouse an employee inadvertently switched two shipping labels. The result is that your order was sent to another customer and vice versa. We have shipped the correct order to you; SureSux will not be charged for the order. If you return the incorrect order (at our expense) we will discount your next order 30 percent.

Rest assured that this will not happen again. In response to this incident, we have changed our procedure. From now on, all orders and shipping labels will be marked with the same bar code. These bar codes must match before we can ship the order.

Buzz, we value your business and look forward to serving you again soon.

Kind Regards,

Al Trublschutte
VP, Customer Care

Figure 5.1 *We rarely saw our customer guru, but Buzz received a letter from him and shared it with Rick. Buzz was impressed at the prompt, specific response.*

food for thought

Gray's Notebook

1. *Imagine that you are a first-time customer of your business. What would you expect in terms of customer service? As things are now, would you get it? If not, why not?*
2. *Identify three places that you patronize because you feel well treated (e.g., shops, restaurants, services). What do they do that makes you feel well treated? Can you borrow any of what they do in your own business?*
3. *What other options do your customers have? Write down the names of your three biggest competitors. What are the greatest assets and liabilities of each?*
4. *What do your customers know they want? Are you offering it to them?*
5. *What don't your customers yet know they want? Look six months into the future. Can you anticipate something that they may need then?*
6. *Do you make your customers' problem your problem and try to fix it? Or do you make your problem their problem?*

Addison's Brain Trust

Wait, there's more! Check out these books for additional information and insight:

> *Relationship Selling* by Jim Cathcart (Perigee, 1990)
> *A Complaint is a Gift* by Janelle Barlow and Claus Moller (Berrett-Koehler, 1996)

S.P. Surfs the Internet

Top reasons why customers stop buying:

- ★ Better product: 15%
- ★ Cheaper product: 15%
- ★ Lack of attention: 20%
- ★ Poor service: 45%

Source: Forum Corporation

Rick's Smart Talk

"Every crowd has a silver lining."

—*P.T. Barnum*

Connie's Smart Questions

Customers complain. It's human nature. Rather than seeing it as a hassle, learn to view gripes as your very own free focus group. You've got to know that Noreen is helping a lot of companies. Is she helping yours? If she shows up griping, ask these questions:

- How do you view customers who complain?
- How does your organization view them?
- Do you keep track of customer complaints? What trends do you see?
- Do you know that often customer complaints that you hear are only the tip of the iceberg? (For every customer who complains, there are several more who feel the same way but don't say anything.)
- How much does it cost you to get new customers?
- Are people trained to deal with customer complaints, or do you "shoot the messenger" and ignore complaints or punish the people who complain?
- What do you do to try to hear from customers who *don't* complain?

Make a note the next time you complain to a business. How did the company respond to the complaint? Can you learn anything from how the other company handled your complaint? Ask yourself: Could any of our customers make the same complaint about us?

Gray's Anatomy of Business

Yes, we all say we are customer focused. But does your company mouth the slogan, or are you really and truly customer focused? First off, do you even know who your most important customers are? Make a list of your top five customers. Why did you choose the ones that you did? Is it because they're the most profitable, because they give you credibility, or because they can open up new industries for your products? Now ask yourself what these customers like about dealing with your organization, what don't they like about dealing with it, and if they had a magic wand, what they would change about your organization or their relationship with it.

Barbie's Brainy Glossary

Business-to-business   Marketing products or services to other businesses, rather than to the public.

Customers   The people who keep us in business. The sun, moon, and stars.

Relationship selling   A sales technique that relies on a long-term working relationship and in-depth knowledge of the customer so that sales are targeted to the customer's specific needs. Like when Joe always sets aside the size 6 Manolo Blahniks for me.

Telephone hell   An electronic system that directs customers to one extension after another, without ever allowing them to resolve their concern or to speak to anyone.

chapter six

Relationships

How to Be a Successful Team Player

The next time you need some great business advice, turn to my favorite guru, Aretha Franklin. Aretha knows R-E-S-P-E-C-T, and I've learned that if you don't show it and don't earn it you won't get much done.

I thought I knew respect. My grandfather was an army general, and when we were at his house we saluted—literally. But it turns out that respect is a little more complicated in business. Respect isn't just showing deference. It's the pillar of every relationship you have, and therefore the pillar of everything you do.

All that became very clear after I almost ruined any chance we had of turning the division around. I was making enemies as fast as I was making friends, and that's because I lost sight of how to be a team player.

Being a Team Player Means Playing Well with Every Member of the Team.

The best team players manage their relationships with three groups simultaneously: those above them, their peers, and (if applicable) those subordinate to them. Most of us focus our efforts on those above us, but we don't always do it effectively.

Working well with your boss (what the business books I read call *managing up*) demands several things. The first is to recognize that your boss doesn't work in a vacuum. It's tempting to think that the boss can do anything he or she likes—and sometimes it may seem that way. But he or she works in the same organization you do, and is subject to the same rules. That means that you'll do better if you look past just doing your tasks well and think about the bigger picture:

- What pressure, history, and politics influence your boss's actions?
- What does your boss expect of you? (Don't just focus on deliverables. Think about politics, standards, behavior, communication, and ethics.)
- What does your boss value? What can you do to support those values?
- How does your boss win? How can you help him or her win?

The best bosses work hard to share this information with their employees. But even the best bosses also face deadlines, political pressure, and a lot of people pulling them in all directions. If your boss doesn't volunteer the answers to these questions, ask.

Maybe this sounds as if it's all about the boss. It isn't. Remember, you're both playing on the same team. If you work at it, you can stop working toward *your* goals or *your boss's* goals and start working toward your *mutual* goals.

My sister, Mauve, is a career food server. She's worked at many kinds of restaurants, and she says that when she has a good relationship with her boss she gets higher tips. How? Well, in coffee shops the goal is to turn tables as fast as possible. When the kitchen is slow getting the food out or the bus staff lets empty tables sit too long piled with dirty dishes, Mauve can go to her boss for help. When he intervenes, he isn't just helping her—he's helping the restaurant and therefore himself.

In a fine dining restaurant, the goal is different. There, the aim is a slow meal and the sale of many extras, such as wine and dessert. In that setting, the boss can help by making sure that all departments are working together to offer great service. When that happens, everybody wins.

The Better Your Relationship with Your Boss, the More You Can Excel.

Of course, you can't support the boss and ignore everybody else. For one thing, a poor relationship with your coworkers actually creates more work for your boss. I found that out when I burned some bridges with Rick. What did he do? He went straight to Virginia. He wasn't wrong—just as in the restaurants, the boss is there to resolve problems. It's better, though, not to be the source of problems that need to be resolved.

It's better still to be the source of solutions to problems. Your odds of success are much greater if you can count on your colleagues. That's hardly news, even to a shy nerd like me. What was news to me, though, was how much I limited myself. I've always thought of my colleagues as just the small circle of people I work with most. But as we worked to reinvent our division, I saw that the circle kept getting bigger. First I noticed that I was getting great help from my kids' babysitter. Then I realized that we were getting ideas and support from customers and vendors.

In short, I've learned that you never know who may offer help or have the answer, the contact, or the resource you need. Improve your odds by extending your circle:

- Who influences your ability to do your job well? How often do you reach out to these customers, vendors, or coworkers? In what ways do you reach out?
- Do you take the time to get to know people who don't work in your department? What doors can they help open? What can they teach you about other parts of the company? What can you teach them about your part of the company?
- Do you do favors without asking for anything in return?

Because I'm shy, I used to wait for others to take the initiative and reach out. Don't make the same mistake.

Develop and Maintain Good Working Relationships outside Your Immediate Circle.

If you manage other people, good relationships with your subordinates will pay off, too. Looking back, I know that I didn't approach Virginia earlier because I didn't really know her. We didn't really have a working relationship. I knew her mostly as a shadowy and scary figure who passed through occasionally—usually with bad news. It may sound crazy, but I didn't really know how to approach her.

After I did make the effort, I saw that Virginia was a pretty surprising person. But we didn't connect until late in the process. If she had been more accessible, I think everything we did would have gone faster because we could have been more direct. Instead, we spent a lot of time second-guessing her and trying to bring her up to speed. As you'll see, never during the whole process of reinventing the division did Virginia come to us to see how we were doing or to offer her support.

Employees Are Unlikely to Walk through Fire for a Boss They Barely Know.

Ultimately, we didn't know or trust that Virginia respected us. Without respect, there isn't much of a relationship. And without relationships there isn't much trust or cooperation. Think where we might be if we had had all that from the beginning.

360-DEGREE FEEDBACK FORM

Sometimes employees are unaware they need to improve a skill because they do not see themselves as others see them. The 360-degree feedback form is an opportunity to give employees candid, respectful feedback. Your responses are confidential, so please be candid. Thank you for your help.

Name of employee receiving feedback: _____ Date: _____

Your relationship to the employee (choose one):

___ Peer   ___ Subordinate   ___ Vendor   ___ Supervisor/Manager   ___ Customer

For each statement, please circle the number that best expresses your experience of the employee.

	NEVER			ALWAYS	
1. The employee meets his/her commitments.	1	2	3	4	5
2. The employee shares information.	1	2	3	4	5
3. The employee supports the team.	1	2	3	4	5
4. I can depend on this employee.	1	2	3	4	5
5. This employee's actions are consistent with what he/she says.	1	2	3	4	5
6. This employee understands my role.	1	2	3	4	5
7. I trust this employee.	1	2	3	4	5
8. This employee shows respect for others.	1	2	3	4	5
9. This employee shares his/her concerns.	1	2	3	4	5
10. This employee treats others fairly.	1	2	3	4	5
11. This employee values excellence.	1	2	3	4	5
12. This employee helps others when necessary.	1	2	3	4	5
13. This employee communicates effectively.	1	2	3	4	5
14. This employee establishes clear priorities.	1	2	3	4	5
15. This employee is able to adapt to change.	1	2	3	4	5

Figure 6.1 *I learned firsthand that how we see ourselves and how others see us are not always the same. When those views are different, it can really hinder effectiveness.*

food for thought

Gray's Notebook

1. *Take a walk in your boss's shoes. What pressure, history, and politics does he or she face? Your boss may seem pretty irrational most of the time. Spend less time complaining and more time studying what your boss does. You may learn a lot about the pressure that your boss is facing from his or her boss.*
2. *How does your boss win? Identify three ways you can help your boss win. Look for places where your boss's interests intersect with your own. The key is not to hold your nose and do what your boss wants, but to find the places where your interests align.*
3. *How often do you reach out to coworkers, vendors, and customers? Make it a point to spend time with one person from each group at least once a month. What can they teach you about your business?*

Addison's Brain Trust

Wait, there's more! Check out these books for additional information and insight:

Reading People by Jo-Ellan Dimitrius (Random House, 1998)
Working Wounded: Advice that Adds Insight to Injury by Bob Rosner (Warner, 2000)

S.P. Surfs the Internet

What is the most important thing to you at work?

- ★ A bigger paycheck: 8%
- ★ Care and concern: 13%
- ★ A chance to contribute: 37%
- ★ Fair treatment: 41%

Source: WorkingWounded.com/ABCnews.com online ballot

Rick's Smart Talk

"Suffer fools gladly. They may be right."

—*Holbrook Jackson*

Connie's Smart Questions

Work is all about relationships. But, in the age of e-mail, many of us are losing our skills for dealing with others. Somebody at work calls these things emotional intelligence. I always called it common sense.

- How much time do you spend with people (not just your key stakeholders at work, but people in general)?
- Do you stop, look, and listen to them? No, I mean *really* listen.
- What can you do to increase your patience and attentiveness?
- Do you reveal something of yourself when you deal with others?
- What are your biases or prejudices when it comes to others?
- What can you do to minimize these biases and prejudices?
- How open-minded are you? Can you learn to more effectively walk in another person's shoes?

Think about your closest relationships outside work—your friends and neighbors. What do you give to those relationships? Do you offer the same things at work? If not, why not? What can you learn from your own example that you can apply at work?

Gray's Anatomy of Business

Many of our key relationships at work are a one-way street: People do stuff for us but we don't reciprocate. You would never let that happen, would you? Make three columns. In the first column, list your 10 most important relationships at work. In the second column, beside each name, write down the last time that person did something that really helped you at work. In the third column, beside each name, write down the last time you went above and beyond the call of duty to help that person. Shouldn't you be doing more to support your key relationships?

Barbie's Brainy Glossary

American idol What you'll become if you manage your relationships effectively. We all work with Paula Abdul.

Enemy Someone who wishes you were dead and vows to make your life a living hell, just like Shana Wilkes did to me after I was picked homecoming queen. In high school I just cried about it. Now I'd try to find common ground and figure out a way to work together.

Reciprocate To give and take in kind. Like when S.P. shows me how to do something in PowerPoint and I show her how to dress better.

Team player Someone who puts the needs of the group or the organization ahead of his or her own and does what he or she can to support others. *Not* a synonym for "never disagreeing."

Part 2

SALES

chapter seven

Sales Autopsy

How to Make Sense of Losing a Key Customer

Our best customers are like cars. At first, when they are new, we pay rapt attention to every detail. We park the new car defensively, we wince at every scratch or ding, and we wash and tune faithfully. We call new customers regularly, we wince at every misstep we make, and we jump to meet every request. Then, at some point, both the car and the customer stop being new and we start taking them for granted. By the time we sell the car, it looks like it's been out of favor a while. By the time we lose the customer, no one much notices—and no one asks why.

I think we lose our enchantment with the car—and the customer—when the work outweighs the novelty. After our friends stop oohing and ahhing, the car still needs gas, tune-ups, washes, and repairs. After the boss stops congratulating us, the new customer still has demands, problems, and questions. The truth is that cars and customers are work. But they are also necessities—and the more we avoid the work, the more work they become.

Keeping Customers Happy Is Work—But Getting New Customers Is More Work.

I've read a lot of articles that talked about how much more it costs to get a new customer than to keep an old one. I never really stopped to think about what that meant, though, until we lost so many customers when Global Gadget was reorganized. The work of taking care of our existing customers really was routine. Getting new customers became all-consuming—we were all working extra hours and taking on more work to make it happen.

I was pretty humbled by the whole experience. Then I found out that losing our biggest customer had triggered the whole move. The loss was so great it literally threatened our survival. Yet none of us could even name the customer. Pathetic, isn't it? We were oblivious to our greatest asset and were doing nothing special at all to keep the customer happy. We knew so little that we had no idea why we lost the customer. When I thought about it, I realized we never knew why our customers left.

Losing Any Customer Should Prompt an Investigation.

It seemed crazy that no one (I was guilty, too) was asking why. Name the last time someone you know let a relationship fall apart without wanting to know why. We always want to know what happened, even if we're just trying to reassure ourselves that it wasn't our fault. Somehow, though, when a customer leaves, people shrug and say, "It's just business."

I don't really know what "It's just business" means. Maybe that's easier for some people than looking for answers; maybe they feel another customer is always waiting. But I remembered what happened just before Sherman got hired. The creative guy we had before that came in one day and quit. Everyone really liked him, and he had done great work. A few days later, Virginia started calling us all into her office to ask why he might have left, whether we were happy, whether we had thoughts of leaving, and things like that. I asked Virginia why she was asking all the questions. She told me that she had been to a seminar in which the speaker pointed out that if a $5,000 piece of equipment disappeared one night, the company would investigate the theft aggressively—and that losing an employee was worth a lot more than $5,000. Isn't a good customer worth a lot more, too?

If someone stole a computer and you found out there was a hole in your security system, you would fix it. We had a big hole in our business now, and I thought we should know why. I didn't want to work hard to get new customers and then make the same mistakes and lose them, too.

That was OK as far as it went, but I should have kept thinking. I should have pursued it myself or had Rick pursue it. Instead, I asked Barbie to do it. Don't misunderstand—I'm not criticizing Barbie. She did a fine job. But I can't believe that the customer felt that his business was too important when he got a call from an intern. Once again, we didn't walk our talk.

Still, even if the way we handled it was imperfect, Barbie did get some good information. What she found out wasn't pretty. Our problems went far deeper than just customer service glitches or billing errors. Instead, our inability to deliver product more quickly was the root issue—and one that would have cost us more customers.

An Investigation Should Lead to Change.

In a sense, we were fortunate because we found out what our reputation was in time to do something about it. We were able to shift the focus of what we were doing and really make some fundamental changes. We were able to use what we learned to get new customers, too.

I really hope I've learned never to take a customer for granted. I'm not taking any for granted now. Instead, I'm using what we learned. I'm not waiting until we lose a customer to ask questions. Instead, I'm taking time after every project or major sale to stop and ask what we learned and what we can do better. I want to solve the next problem *before* it costs us a customer.

I'm doing the same with my car, too. It may not be new, but I'm acting as if it is.

script for autopsy calls

Losing a client is a serious concern. It's a revenue loss. But it also means that we have failed to meet our client's expectations. We need to understand what happened so that we can improve our business. Use this script as a guide when calling clients who have announced that they are taking their business elsewhere.

Good [morning, afternoon], this is [your name] with Global Gadget. Our goal is to surpass our customers' expectations, and we're concerned that we've fallen short of that goal. I would appreciate it if you would please take a few minutes to let us know how we can better serve our customers.

Ideally, the contact will agree to talk with you. If the contact declines, offer to call at a more convenient time. If the client agrees to talk, proceed.

- What is the **primary** reason you chose another gadget supplier (e.g., price, product quality, product design, delivery time)?
- Were there other reasons that influenced your decision?
- Even if we were ultimately unable to offer you a comparable deal (e.g., match another supplier's price), do you feel that Global Gadget made a sincere effort to offer you the deal you wanted?
  Yes, my salesperson cared about my business and tried to keep it.
  No, no one cared about my business.
  Generally, would you say that your salesperson understood your business? (If no, what do you wish the salesperson had better understood?)
- Overall, how would you describe the quality of Global Gadget's products?
  Excellent   Good   Fair   Poor
- Overall, how would you describe the quality of Global Gadget's service?
  Excellent   Good   Fair   Poor
- Is there anything we can do to win back your business?

Thank the customer for his or her time. Tell the customer again how much we value their business.

Within two business days of the call, send a letter in the mail (not e-mail) thanking them for their time.

copy'n clip

Figure 7.1 *After we lost our biggest customer and almost lost other clients, Rick put together this script so that everyone on the sales team would call former clients and make sure that we were aware of all the issues we needed to address.*

food for thought

Gray's Notebook

1. *Identify formerly profitable customers who are no longer customers. Ask them why they've left and if there was any way you could've kept their business.*

2. *Don't debate or defend your point of view—just listen. Write down five points the customer raises. Do any surprise you? If so, what could you have done to identify the problem earlier? If none surprise you, why haven't you taken action? Is there something you could have done, or is the issue beyond your control?*

3. *How can you apply what you've learned so you don't have to lose any more key customers? List three steps that you will take within the next month.*

4. *Thank former customers for their business and leave the door open to work with them again. Check with them in 90 days to see if they are happy with their new supplier.*

Addison's Brain Trust

Wait, there's more! Check out these books for additional information and insight:

Selling 2.0 by Josh Gordon (Berkeley, 2000)
A Complaint Is a Gift by Janelle Barlow (Berrett-Koehler, 1996)

S.P. Surfs the Internet

A survey asked salespeople who had lost accounts during the previous year what went wrong; the customers who took their business elsewhere were then asked the same questions. Surprise! Salespeople and their customers don't always see things the same way.

* ★ The competition offered a better price: 62% of customers agree, 55% of salespeople agree
* ★ There were too many problems: 58% of customers agree, 21% of salespeople agree
* ★ Quality deteriorated: 43% of customers agree, 17% of salespeople agree
* ★ The competition built a relationship with the customer: 43% of customers agree, 19% of salespeople agree
* ★ Too little attention was paid to customers: 28% of customers agree, 28% of salespeople agree

Source: Selling 2.0 by Josh Gordon (Berkeley, 2000)

Rick's Smart Talk

"Whom the gods want to destroy they send 40 years of success."   —*Anonymous*

Connie's Smart Questions

I like watching figure skating competitions on TV. Sometimes the skaters who make the fewest mistakes win medals. Other times, the skaters who skate best win. And sometimes the medals are decided by something else, such as an injury. Sales is like that, too. Sometimes salespeople lose business, and other times someone else wins it or the competition changes in some way. Which is true for you? Ask yourself:

- Are new competitors entering the market?
- Are your competitors selling their products at below cost to grab market share?
- Have your customers gone out of business?
- Are your customers changing their business model?
- Are your customers shrinking their operations?
- Are your customers' customers hurting?

Look for patterns. How can you counter changes in your market?

Gray's Anatomy of Business

When calling former customers, act like Lt. Columbo. Show real curiosity and interest. Ask simple questions. And play dumb if you have to. Just get as much information as you can and never argue with what they're telling you. Practice being Lt. Columbo with your kids and family and then try it on former customers. Always hone your routine with smaller customers and work up to the more important ones.

Barbie's Brainy Glossary

Complaints Expressions of dissatisfaction. Sometimes voiced about trivia, but more often only expressed after problems have become serious. Each one represents only a sampling of customers with similar concerns.

Delivery time The time between when you place an order and when you receive it. Usually measured in days, but when you place a catalog order for something you *really* want it's measured in hours.

Former customers People or businesses that used to pay your bills. Also known as future customers, if you are smart.

Retention Holding secure. In sales, it refers to the customers you keep.

chapter eight

Know Your Market

How to Understand What the Market Wants So You Can Deliver

Everything I know about sizing up a market I learned from selling Girl Scout cookies. I suppose it would be more accurate to say I learned from watching girls sell Girl Scout cookies. Anyway, when Violet was a Girl Scout I learned that when your scout sells, you *all* sell. I have to say we sold a lot of cookies—enough that I don't care if ever see another Thin Mint.

Sorry—I digress. The girls are encouraged to sell door-to-door. But Taupe was working crazy hours *and* she's a marketing professional, so the idea of selling door-to-door lasted about two minutes.

We were sitting around the dinner table one evening when Taupe challenged Violet to think about how she was going to sell the cookies. Violet, of course, wanted to be a sales star and sell about a million boxes. Taupe didn't laugh. Instead, she got out a calculator and had Violet run some numbers. Violet figured out that if every person in town bought two boxes she still wouldn't be even halfway to a million. Violet was the first to admit that not everyone would buy two boxes ("I met someone once who doesn't like the cookies," she said earnestly), so she surrendered dreams of a million. "Maybe 100," she said.

Know How Many Buyers Are in Your Market.

Did I remember that lesson when we were searching for new customers for our gadgets? No. Instead, I was following Rick's lead and looking at our prospects from the wrong perspective entirely. After losing a big account, Rick wanted to replace it with another big account. I was nervous about putting all our eggs in one basket again, so I wasn't convinced that one big customer was a good idea.

But neither of us could define the universe of potential buyers. We didn't know how many companies buy the kind of products we produce. Without that information our numbers were just as much a fantasy as Violet's million boxes of cookies. Not only didn't we know how many gadgets we potentially could sell, we had to figure out market share. In theory, Rick could sell his one big client and we would still have missed 98 percent of the potential market.

Not only did we not know how many buyers there were, we had no idea what they bought. Did each prospect represent a buyer of 1 type of gadget, or 12, or 112? Violet assumed that each buyer would enjoy two kinds of cookies. Were our numbers any more realistic? We also didn't know how often our customers bought. Would these prospects buy gadgets once and never be heard from again? Or would they place an order every week? Violet knew she had a limited time in which she could sell cookies; we were acting as if we also had limited time. It would make more sense to pursue repeat buyers, but we didn't know who they were.

Know How Much Your Prospects Buy—and How Often.

I felt pretty stupid when I asked Taupe's advice (she is a marketing pro, after all) and she reminded me of these basic questions. In retrospect, I think the reorganization made us all panic a little. We were in such a hurry to do *something* that we weren't being smart about what we were doing. (I'm sure nothing like that has ever happened in your company.)

Happily for me, I didn't get Taupe's entire lecture on the principles of marketing. But later, as I was trying to fall asleep by counting boxes of cookies, I remembered some other lessons from our days as cookie pushers.

Taupe asked Violet when she was most likely to think about food. Violet rattled off a bunch of situations—at the movies, on sleepovers, at ball games, after school, on holidays. "OK," Taupe said. "How about when someone rings your doorbell and interrupts you?"

"Not so much," Violet answered. "Oh! I get it! You mean that we'd sell more if we didn't go door-to-door." Taupe didn't say anything, but I could see from the look in her eyes that she was already planning Violet's career in marketing. So they sold cookies at the movies, at ball games, and after school at the bus stop. Violet didn't sell a million boxes, but she did sell more than anyone else in her troop.

Know How Your Buyers Behave.

I knew we weren't going to find gadget buyers at the movies or at ball games—at least not buyers who would buy in grosses. But the memories reminded me of what else we needed to know. Just knowing how many potential buyers there were wasn't enough. Who were they buying from now? Did they have long-term contracts with their suppliers, or were they buying one order at a time? What was driving their choice—price, selection, financing options, delivery time? We needed many more answers.

I knew that Rick would resist even asking the questions. It's not that Rick isn't smart, or that he's a bad guy. He's just a salesperson, and so he never, ever wants to hear any variation of "no." But asking the questions means that you find out some prospects are not really buyers, and that means that you've said "no" for them.

Still, we were running out of time and we had to find the people most likely to say "yes." We needed to know who our market was. Without that information, I knew we would fail—because that's the way the cookie crumbles.

food for thought

Gray's Notebook

1. *What is the universe of your market? How many buyers are there? To answer that question, first define your market. For example, suppose you own a Thai restaurant. One way to define your market is to include everyone who lives in or visits your town. But that's not realistic. Some people don't like Thai food or don't know what it is. Others may not be able to afford your restaurant or may be unwilling to make the drive required. Some simply don't know about your restaurant.*

2. *How is the universe changing? Find out whether your market is growing or contracting. Are more people moving into your town, or is the population stable? How many other restaurants are vying for your customers? How has that changed in the last year?*

3. *How do potential buyers behave? Do some research about restaurant-goers in your town. (In this case, the local chamber of commerce or a restaurant association could probably help you. Think about similar sources of information in your market.) Find out how these diners behave. How often do they dine out? How far do they drive? How much do they spend? Who dines—adults only, or families with their children? The more you know, the better you can market to them.*

4. *How can you change the market? You can raise awareness simply by advertising. That may not be enough to get people to try Thai food, however. You could offer free samples or Thai cooking classes. What can you do to change your market?*

Addison's Brain Trust

Wait, there's more! Check out these books for additional information and insight:

The Accidental Salesperson by Chris Lytle (Amacom, 2000)
High Performance Selling by Terry Beck (Career Press, 2001)

S.P. Surfs the Internet

What characteristics of a salesperson earn a customer's trust? Customers and salespeople aren't too far apart in their perspectives.

★ Knows product: 79% of customers agree, 76% of salespeople agree
★ Understands business: 63% of customers agree, 73% of salespeople agree
★ Is reliable: 63% of customers agree, 75% of salespeople agree

★ Understands needs: 63% of customers agree, 85% of salespeople agree
★ Has confidence in product: 54% of customers agree, 63% of salespeople agree

Source: Selling 2.0 *by Josh Gordon (Berkeley, 2000)*

Rick's Smart Talk

"You can make more friends in two months by becoming more interested in other people than you can in two years by trying to get other people interested in you."

—*Dale Carnegie*

Connie's Smart Questions

One time my kids were watching a movie called *Big* on TV. In the movie, a boy was trapped inside a man's body. He became a big star at a toy company because he was the only one who looked at toys the way children look at them. There's a lesson in that for all of us.

- Do you view the world through the eyes of your customers?
- What are their biggest headaches and opportunities?
- What social or business trends are affecting your customer's business?
- What can you do to better inform your customers about your industry?

Take the answers to these questions and write an essay describing your market. Now that you know how your customers see things, how can you position your product or service as a benefit to them?

Gray's Anatomy of Business

We get so focused on our customers that we forget they have customers, too. Take a few moments to make a list of your 10 most important customers (you determine the criteria for "most important," such as profitability, prestige, and so on). Now, list each of *their* three biggest customers. Chances are you'll be more successful if you keep in mind how you can help your customer look good for the people paying their bills. For example, if you are in sales for a hotel chain, you could strengthen your sales by making your corporate travel contacts look good.

Barbie's Brainy Glossary

Big fish   The most desirable conquest. In sales, the client with the most to spend. In high school, the captain of the football team.

Market   A category of potential buyers. Vegetarians (like S.P.) are a market for tofu.

Prospecting   The process of identifying potential buyers. Similar to the process of arriving at a party and deciding who you are willing to talk with.

chapter nine

Qualifying

How to Identify Your Most Likely Buyers

Hurry dating is wasted on romance; it's much better suited to sales.

You've probably heard about hurry dating. The idea is that a bunch of singles gather together in a big room, such as a hotel ballroom. They sit opposite each other and talk, but only for three minutes. Then a bell rings and everybody shifts so they can have the next three-minute conversation. It continues long enough for people to have many conversations before the evening is up. The idea is that three minutes is long enough for you to decide whether the person you're talking with is someone you find interesting. If so, you can arrange a real date. If not, you've lost only three minutes, not a whole evening. S.P. swears by it.

The person I wish swore by it is Rick. I'm not talking about his dating habits—I couldn't care less about those. What I mean is that three minutes spent talking with a prospect is three minutes more than most get now, and we'd all be better off.

If Rick looks at his computer database and sees that there are 125 names in it, then he believes he has 125 prospects. But he doesn't. Even after all we've been through, that's still true.

All Prospects Are Not Equal. Some Are More Likely to Buy than Others.

Suppose you are a realtor and you hold an open house one Saturday to showcase one of your listings. Let's assume 40 people tour the home during the open house. Are they all equally likely to buy? Of course not. Some are merely looky-loos who have no interest in buying any home. Some people can't afford the home; others want something larger, or smaller, or with different features. In truth, none of the 40 people may be a likely buyer.

The same thing is true no matter what you're selling. Granted, the best salespeople can sell to prospects who didn't start out inclined to buy. But even if they succeed, it will take longer and their conversion rate (the number of completed sales of the total attempted) will be lower than if they only sold to those likeliest to buy. If you were a salesperson, wouldn't you rather pursue a sale that was closer to a sure thing?

Rick denies it, but I'm convinced that he's waiting for someone to distill a magic potion to help him identify buyers. Or maybe he's scouring the listings on eBay for a crystal ball. My sense is that he'll do anything to avoid asking questions, which is the best way there is to identify likely buyers. The experts call his process *qualifying*.

The Best Way to Identify Buyers Is to Ask Questions—Lots of Questions.

For a long time earlier in her career, Taupe managed salespeople. She tells me that most of them avoid asking questions because they are afraid that asking questions offers prospects the opportunity to say "no." The theory is that until they've said "no," they can still be considered a potential "yes."

But Taupe says that some prospects are always going to say "no"—no salesperson has 100 percent success. If you accept that, then the faster someone says "no," the better, because it means you can stop wasting your time and focus on the people who may say "yes."

Sometimes you can tell a prospect will never become a buyer after just a few questions. Imagine again that you are a realtor. You've had 40 people attend your open house. Suppose you asked each one of them these questions:

- Are you in the market for a home?
- Are you planning on buying a home within the next month or two?
- What price range are you able to afford?
- Is buying a home contingent on selling your current home?

Some people will not know the answers to these questions, but most will. I don't have a real estate license, but I know that people who answer "yes" to the first question merit more of my attention than the people who answer "no."

Once people have made the first cut and are generally qualified, you can qualify them further by asking more specific questions. That's the time to ask how large a house they want, which features are important, what sort of neighborhood they prefer, and so on.

Of course, we don't sell houses. We sell gadgets, so the questions we asked were specific to us:

- Do you use gadgets in any of the products you produce?
- If so, do you buy those gadgets from an outside source?
- What gadgets are you currently buying? In what quantity? How often?

And so forth.

The Better You Understand What Your Customer Wants, the Better Able You Will Be to Give it to Him or Her—or to Know that You Can't.

This process isn't as mercenary as it may sound. It is about making sales. But it's also about helping customers.

As you ask questions, you want to ask about more than just buying habits. You want to know the business issues prospects face—the challenges, the problems, the things they worry about. It may be that you have the tool to help them overcome their challenge, or you have the solution to their problem, or you can alleviate their worry.

Suppose their profits are being squeezed because their competitor offers a cheaper product and so they've cut their prices. If you can help them produce their product for less, you have solved their problem. Alternatively, if they are losing sales because of a reputation for poor quality, you may be able to help them improve their quality. Whatever the issue, if you can help it's a win-win sale. If you help solve a problem, you have a much stronger sale—one more likely to result in a more satisfied customer, renewed business, and longer-term profitability.

Win-Win Sales Are the Strongest Sales.

When we first started our long process of turning the division around, we had a lot of prospects and none at all. That's because we weren't asking the right questions. After we did start asking questions—and getting answers—we changed our goal. We stopped going after sales and started looking for partners. We focused on a small but crucial pool of prospects.

Once we knew who we were pursuing and why, even Rick found it easy to ask the final qualifying question: What will it take for you to try our gadgets?

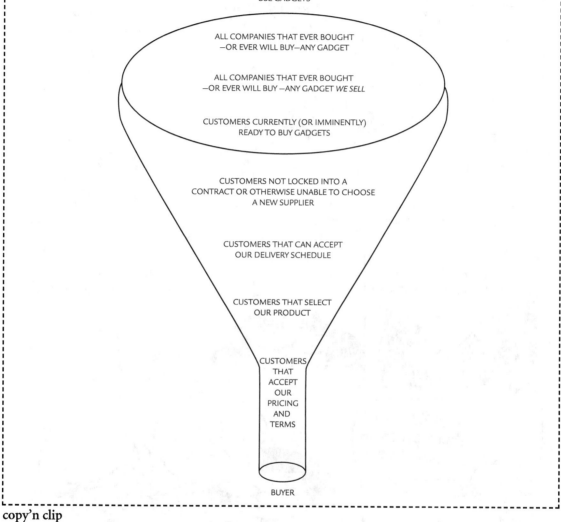

RICK'S QUALIFYING FUNNEL

COMPANIES THAT DO NOT
USE GADGETS

ALL COMPANIES THAT EVER BOUGHT
—OR EVER WILL BUY—ANY GADGET

ALL COMPANIES THAT EVER BOUGHT
—OR EVER WILL BUY —ANY GADGET *WE SELL*

CUSTOMERS CURRENTLY (OR IMMINENTLY)
READY TO BUY GADGETS

CUSTOMERS NOT LOCKED INTO A
CONTRACT OR OTHERWISE UNABLE TO CHOOSE
A NEW SUPPLIER

CUSTOMERS THAT CAN ACCEPT
OUR DELIVERY SCHEDULE

CUSTOMERS THAT SELECT
OUR PRODUCT

CUSTOMERS
THAT
ACCEPT
OUR
PRICING
AND
TERMS

BUYER

Figure 9.1 *Initially, Rick was focused on a very small pool of prospects, all of them big companies. He was betting that he could replace Kitchen Cartel with a similar customer. Eventually, he decided that he needed to pursue many more clients and better qualify them. He developed his funnel diagram as a reminder for himself, and later shared it with the other salespeople.*

food for thought

Gray's Notebook

1. Who isn't currently buying from you who should be buying? Why should they be? Do you offer the right price, features they need, more convenient financing terms, or some other clear benefit?

2. Why aren't they buying from you now? Are your prices or terms prohibitive? Are they locked into a contract with another supplier? Are they honoring a long-term business relationship? Find out what's driving their buying.

3. Can you solve a problem for your prospects, make them more productive, or help them better serve their customers? What do you need to know to answer those questions? Make a list of 10 questions to pose to your prospects. If you had the answers to those questions, could you tailor a sales pitch to them?

4. What would it take for prospects to try your product or service? Can you offer a discount, better financing, or more extensive customer support?

Addison's Brain Trust

Wait, there's more! Check out these books for additional information and insight:

Proactive Selling by William Miller (Amacom, 2003)
Questions that Work by Andrew Finlayson (Amacom, 2001)

S.P. Surfs the Internet

What's the toughest part of a sale?

- ★ Overcoming objections: 16%
- ★ Getting prospects to sign on the dotted line: 41%
- ★ Getting your foot in the door: 42%

Source: WorkingWounded.com/ABCnews.com online ballot

Rick's Smart Talk

"You can't sing songs if you ain't got nothin' to say."

—*Willie Nelson*

Connie's Smart Questions

My sister owns a bakery. Every time I'm out with her she makes us stop anywhere they sell baked goods. We have to check out what they make, how they decorate things, what their prices are, and so on. She wants to know how everyone else is doing things. She uses what she learns, too. She is always trying new things in her own shop. Ask yourself:

- Who are our competitors?
- What do they do well?
- How do they get their customers?
- How do they keep their customers?
- How are their products better than ours?
- How are their products worse than ours?

Study your competitors' ads—in the telephone book, in the newspaper, on the radio, anywhere you can find them. What can you learn from them? Make a list of everything your competitors are promoting (e.g., price, hours, service). What can you learn from their ads? Which ad appeals to you most? Why?

Gray's Anatomy of Business

Once I heard about Ikea's efforts to find new employees. They found that all the usual avenues (such as classified ads and agencies) were dead ends. So they started advertising on the bathroom walls of restaurants. Unconventional, yes, but everyone's got to go. So where do your customers and potential customers gather? Come up with at least three new places to target potential customers. For each one, specify how you would attract their attention in the environment you've chosen.

Barbie's Brainy Glossary

Betty Ford   Former First Lady (wife of President Gerald Ford) and the driving force behind the Betty Ford Center, a well-known rehabilitation center.

Qualifying   Identifying prospects that meet specific standards. Like when my Mom points out "appropriate" boys at the country club.

chapter ten

Walk in Their Shoes

*How to Understand the Business Challenges Your Customers Face—
and How You Can Help*

I treasure the moment when Violet conceded that it's possible Taupe and I are not complete idiots. It happened when she finished a school assignment. The kids were supposed to get some sense of the responsibilities of parenthood, so the teacher gave them each a "baby" (a large sack of flour) and made them carry it everywhere and take care of it for a week. When it was over, Violet told us that while she didn't think we were very good at it, parenting *is* hard. (It's the small gifts that matter most.)

While we were struggling to save our division, I sure wanted to give Rick a sack of flour. I thought maybe it would remind him to try to see things the way other people see them. Too often, he tried to close sales for selfish reasons ("I need to meet my quota.") instead of for reasons that matter to the customer. He forgot to walk in their shoes.

You and Your Customers Live in Parallel Universes, and It Pays to Visit Theirs.

I've learned that we want customers to see a very small universe in which we are the only solution to their problems or the only provider of what they need. We want them to rely on us. If they don't, we run the risk that we will lose some or all of their business.

Customers want almost the direct opposite. Customers want to explore several options. They want to know that they are getting the best deal and the most advantageous terms. They want to know that they are doing what is ultimately best for their business.

It's very hard to sell effectively if you don't know anything about the atmosphere or the rules of gravity in the customer's universe. But if you make the effort to see things from their perspective, it gets much easier. Think of it this way: How much can you sell anyone if you don't speak the same language? The "language" in this case is their business reality.

Start by Exploring Their Competitive Position.

No business exists in a vacuum, so it's best to start by understanding their rules of engagement. Does the customer dominate its market or are they a minor player? What's its market share? What does it see is its greatest opportunity for growth—and which of its competitors stand in the way?

Maybe you're wondering why any of this matters, since you can't change it anyway. It matters because it's possible you can change it. Suppose, for example, you are a restaurant supplier. One of your customers is a burger chain that is number two in the market. You have a vegetarian patty that you have never marketed to the chain because it doesn't have a veggie burger on the menu. In meeting with the customer, however, you learn that they are about to enter the California market. Their market research shows that many customers there want veggie burgers. If you can sell to them, you could help them open the new market and increase their market share.

A big factor in whether you get that business is your competition and how the customer perceives it. If other vendors are seen as more reliable, easier to work with, less expensive, or offering a better veggie patty, then you'll have a hard time making the sale. But you'll have no chance if you don't know the customer's perceptions and counter them or make changes to improve what you offer.

Customers Don't Always Know What They Want. But You Might.

Perhaps your burger chain customer has no plan to enter a new market and add a veggie burger to the menu. But the customer is trying to figure out how to improve market share. You're the restaurant supplier, so you work with many restaurants. You can see what's working for other restaurants and what isn't. You can spot trends and be among the first to hear about new ideas. In other words, you're an expert.

That expertise, and what you've learned about the customer's business, makes it possible for you to think about *their* business as if it were *your* business. Imagine yourself as the CEO of your customer's firm. What would you do differently? Which opportunities would you exploit? Then think about your company can help realize those goals and suggest them.

Ultimately, you can't sell something people don't want or need. It's better to move beyond being just a salesperson and become an ally—a business partner. When I look back at what we did, that's just how we changed, without even thinking about it. We stopped thinking about how many gadgets we were trying to sell and started thinking about how we could work with our customers. Thinking in those broader terms also made it easier for us to find ways to fix some of our own problems.

Share What You Know about Your Own Company.

Awareness of our problems and strengths is a good thing. It turns out that sometimes walking in the customer's shoes means talking about you. That sounds contradictory, but it isn't. You will always know much more about your own operation than your customers ever will. That means that you know much more about how things are done in your company—what you can offer and how to maneuver through the system. If you share that information, you can help the customer get more out of working with you.

As you'll see, we really used that technique to our advantage. We took an outdated method of packaging—a method that annoyed many of our customers—and found a situation in which it was a benefit to a potential customer. It never would have happened if we hadn't shared something of our reality, even though we thought it would be seen as negative.

Selling, like parenthood, is tough. At least as parents we have the benefit of having been children and having some idea what the world looks like through their eyes. If you walk in their shoes, you can find out how your customers see the world, too.

BARBIE & S.P. RETURN TO GLOBAL GADGET TO REPORT ON WHAT THEY'VE LEARNED..
BLa Bla Hellish BLa BL BLa BLa BLa BLa Bla La Summer Camp BLa BL BLa BLa BLa BLa BLa Boot Camp BLa BLa
Pedicure Bla BLa BLa
Wait! Wait! Wait! What did they think of GLOBAL GADGET?
Upp & Cummings thinks GLOBAL has the best quality.
So does Midsize.
But they complain about our slow delivery time.
Same here, plus they think we don't care.
Things have to change around here.
What else did you find out?
Find out what your prospects think about your competitors.

food for thought

Gray's Notebook

1. See the world from your customers' perspectives—what are their concerns, who are their competitors, and what opportunities should they be pursuing?
2. What do your customers see as your major competitors' pros and cons? Do you think their assessment is accurate, or do you think they have incorrect information? Can you match the pros they see in your competitor? If not, do you offer other, comparable benefits? Do you and your competitor share the same cons? If not, can you offer a better deal?
3. What can you offer your customers that isn't already being offered to them?
4. Is there something you can offer them that they'd love—or something that they haven't even realized they'd love? For example, the concept of frequent flier miles was a bonanza for the airlines when they were introduced; the programs rewarded business travelers for their loyalty, but travelers hadn't known to ask for such a program.

Addison's Brain Trust

Wait, there's more! Check out these books for additional information and insight:

> Business: The Ultimate Resource (Perseus, 2002)
> Selling for Dummies by Tom Hopkins (IDG, 2001)

S.P. Surfs the Internet

Top reasons why customers stop buying:

- ★ Better product: 15%
- ★ Cheaper product: 15%
- ★ Lack of attention: 20%
- ★ Poor service: 45%

Source: Forum Corporation

Rick's Smart Talk

"In every instance we found that the best-run companies stay as close to the customer as possible."
—Tom Peters

Connie's Smart Questions

When I first got to the U.S. and I was learning English, I kept hearing one word that I didn't understand at all. I tried looking it up and asking my kids. No matter how I spelled it, I couldn't find it in the dictionary. My kids didn't know. Finally, I just asked someone at work. They laughed and laughed. It turns out it wasn't a word at all. I was hearing *WIIFM*. It stands for *what's in it for me*. That's one American phrase I've never forgotten! It's a good one to remember. Ask yourself:

- What is most important to my customers (e.g., money, recognition)?
- What helps them do a better job?
- What obstacles or headaches are they grappling with?
- What value could I bring to them?
- How could I help them to be more successful?

Choose one of your favorite businesses—a shop, restaurant, theater, or anything. Make a list of the things the business does to show you it understands your perspective. Would your business benefit by copying one of those things?

Gray's Anatomy of Business

Too many of us spend too much time communicating via e-mail. When was the last time you visited your major customer at his or her location? Have you seen how your product or service is used by the customer? Can you actually spend a day on the front lines to talk to the people as they use your products? When you limit your interactions to its purchasing department and don't take the time to talk to the end user, you are probably letting new sales opportunities fall through the cracks.

Barbie's Brainy Glossary

Co-branding   A marketing strategy in which two companies jointly market their products or services to their mutual advantage.

End user   The ultimate consumer of a product or service. We sell gadgets to appliance makers, but the end user is the person who buys the appliance.

Googled   Used the Google search engine to research something.

Market position   The niche established for a product, service, or brand name. The market position is how we know we'll never find Tiffany at the discount centers.

Supplier   A firm that provides raw materials or products. We are a supplier of gadgets to appliance manufacturers.

chapter eleven

Objections

How to Identify—and Overcome—the Primary Reasons Your Customers Say "No"

If you want to know how to deal with objections during the sales process, study children as they pursue what they want. Whether they are after a Happy Meal, a new toy, or the chance to stay up late, they have expert technique.

What can we learn from them? We can learn to anticipate objections. We can learn to stay focused. And we can learn to listen.

Those are lessons that many salespeople have yet to learn. I'm sure that at some point you've been buying a car or an insurance policy and raised some sort of objection—and surprised the salesperson.

Children rarely let that happen. They anticipate the objections even before you make them, and they counter them. Not long ago, Kelly wanted to invite a friend to stay to dinner. Right on the heels of asking permission, he told us that it was all right with his friend's mother, that he'd already finished his homework, and that he'd help with the dishes. He neutralized the objections before they ever really had life. After that, we would have had to really scramble to find a good reason not to let the friend stay. The more we worked at it, the more churlish we would seem. Besides, his counters to any possible objections were good ones.

It's a rare salesperson who will raise an objection before the customer does. Think about the times you've bought a car. Has the salesperson ever said, "It's true that this car doesn't get very good gas mileage, but . . ." or "This model's reliability record is just so-so, but . . ."? They wait for you to raise the issue—and hope that you don't. It's not a good strategy, because they leave the elephant in the middle of the room and force you to ask about it. You can only wonder what else they aren't saying.

The Best Defense Is a Good Offense.

When children want something, they focus their energy with laser beam precision. They are relentless in pursuit of the candy, the toy, or staying up late.

Adults aren't always so focused. For example, on Customer Appreciation Day, Rick found out that we had a reputation for slow delivery. That shouldn't have changed anything. The quality of our gadgets was as high as ever. Our delivery time was no slower than it always had been. In fact, after that day it was getting better because of the changes we were making. The only thing that changed was Rick's perception. He began to doubt. In his mind we became The Company that Has Slow Delivery instead of The Company that Makes the Best Gadgets. In other words, Rick started representing a different company.

Salespeople represent their employers in a profound way—the company's identity is also their identity. If the identity changes, it's harder to counter objections. For example, imagine that you're debating about a political issue. You've prepared well, and you know the points that you want to make. Now, imagine that halfway through the debate you are asked to switch and argue the other side. You could do it, but it would be awkward and unpolished at first.

That's what happened to Rick. He later told me that he stopped making calls because they became awkward. Don't allow yourself to be distracted.

Remember Who You Work For.

Staying focused has another benefit, too: It makes it easier to listen. Even if you can't do anything about their concerns, customers want to know that you have heard them. I learned that by watching Taupe when we were house hunting. Taupe had pretty specific ideas about what she wanted, and she gave a list to our real estate agent. The agent checked out what was available and then started showing us some places. At the first few homes, Taupe would spot something she didn't like and fixate on it. She'd mention several times how much she disliked something, and each time the agent would respond by telling her all the features the home had that matched Taupe's list. It isn't like Taupe to be so negative, so finally I asked what she was doing. "I just want to be sure she really understands what we want," she said.

I don't think Taupe is alone. Few of us are eager to make mistakes, and we're even less eager to make big mistakes. The more there is at stake, the more we want reassurance that we aren't doing something hideously wrong.

Since then, I've thought about Taupe's strategy when the kids want something. Take Kelly's request to have his friend stay to dinner. Kelly's friend is a nice kid, so I had no reason to say no. Kelly was sharp and beat me to the punch by countering my objections before I raised them. But if he hadn't neutralized my concerns, I would have asked him whether his friend had permission and whether he had done his homework. It occurred to me that I wasn't looking for a way to say "no." I was looking for a way to say "yes" without making a big mistake.

Objections Are Requests For more Information.

Remember, it's hardly possible for your customers to know too much. The better they understand exactly what they are getting, the stronger the sale will be. Use the process of working through objections. Your customers are.

t r a i n i n g   d e p a r t m e n t

Overcoming Objections: Diagnosis Form

How successful would you be in selling to an invisible client? Odds are, not very. Yet many salespeople may as well be selling to invisible people because they don't fully understand their prospects' situation or objections. You can't overcome an objection you don't know about. Use this diagnosis form to fully explore the objections that your prospects raise. After your initial sales call, write down all your prospects' objections. Then, for each one, ask yourself the questions posed here. If you know the answers, write them down. If you don't know the answers, think about how you can get the information. Go into your follow-up call with a plan to get the information you need. Once you really understand the prospects' objections, counter them.

Sample

Objection: <u>Your product costs too much.</u>

What are they really saying? *Is this really about money? Or is it about value?*

Why are they saying it? *Are they really sharing their budget with you, or letting you know that they can afford it later, in a new budget cycle? Are they letting you know that your competitor's product is less expensive?*

What aren't they saying? *Is it about money or is it about their authority to buy? Or is the money issue just a stall tactic?*

What's your plan? *Get the specifics of what they can afford—and when. Demonstrate the value of your product. Find ways to show that the benefits extend beyond just having the product (e.g., it saves time).*

Objection #1

What are they really saying?

Why are they saying it?

What aren't they saying?

What's your plan?

Objection #2

What are they really saying?

Why are they saying it?

What aren't they saying?

What's your plan?

. . . and so forth

Figure 11.1 *After Rick lost his nerve to face objections, he asked the training department for help. They came up with these guidelines; all our sales consultants use this now. Every sale is different, but these questions are a place to start.*

food for thought

Gray's Notebook

1. *Give customers a chance to fully express their objections. Keep asking questions until you completely understand their concern.*
2. *The best defense is a good offense. List the three objections you hear most often about your product or service. For each objection, write down a counter to the objection.*
3. *Create a grid. Down one side, list the objections that customers raise. Then, next to each objection, write down the demographics of the customer raising the objection. For example, if you are selling big-screen televisions, you might find that women object most to the price while men complain about inadequate features. Can you identify a pattern in the objections? If so, does the pattern offer you a new marketing opportunity? If you owned a restaurant, for example, and parents said that your prices were too high for family dining, you might create a lower-priced children's menu.*
4. *Think about the most recent major purchase you made. Make a list of the objections you raised before you decided to buy. Beside each one, write down how the salesperson overcame your objection. Can your firm use any of those techniques?*

Addison's Brain Trust

Wait, there's more! Check out these books for additional information and insight:

Delivering Knock-Your-Socks-Off Service by Performance Research Associates (Amacom, 2003)

Why People Don't Buy Things: Five Proven Steps to Connect with Your Customers and Dramatically Increase Your Sales by Harry Washburn and Kim Wallace (Perseus, 1999)

S.P. Surfs the Internet

What song do you sing when confronted with a difficult customer?

- ★ "I'll Never Say Goodbye": 13.2%
- ★ "I'll Close My Eyes": 20.7%
- ★ "I'll Be There": 66%

Source: WorkingWounded.com/ABCnews.com online ballot

Rick's Smart Talk

"A little reciprocity goes a long way."

—Malcolm Forbes

Connie's Smart Questions

Go straight to the source. That's what I learned getting my visa to come to the United States. I've used that lesson a lot in my job in the warehouse, too. Do you remember Customer Appreciation Day? Mr. Bravado never would have gotten the solution to his problem about our packaging if he hadn't come to me—I'm the one who could do something for him. It's the same in sales; make sure you are following the right channels. Ask yourself:

- Is it the wrong time for them to buy?
- Are you talking to the wrong person?
- Are you working with the wrong department?
- Are you asking the wrong questions?
- Are you taking the wrong approach?

Each time you get off track, ask yourself what went wrong. For example, if you ended up talking to the wrong person, how did that happen? Were you referred to the wrong person, or did you pursue the wrong person? For each thing that went wrong, figure out a way to do it differently next time—and then follow through.

Gray's Anatomy of Business

Can you turn customers' objections from a solitary struggle to a team-building effort? Bring your group together to identify the Dirty Dozen Customer Complaints. The 12 should be the complaints most likely to cost you business. Give a prize to each person who identifies one of the dozen complaints. Then, as a group, brainstorm ways to address them. Update your Dirty Dozen list, and the strategies to address the complaints, regularly.

Barbie's Brainy Glossary

Distribution channel   The path for getting a product into the hands of consumers. Tupperware's primary distribution channel is in-home sales.

Guarantee   An assurance of quality, often with the promise of a refund if a product or service doesn't meet quality standards.

Objections   Reasons or arguments against a position. For example, my objection to a certain dress might be that it's not cute enough.

Price break   A discount off the price normally charged. You get a price break on makeup when you buy the whole kit instead of one item at a time.

chapter twelve

Secondary Objections

*How to Identify and Overcome the Unspoken—
and Often Emotional—Reasons Customers Say "No"*

Secondary objections are the icebergs in the sea of sales. That's what Rick told us. He said they lurk mostly beneath the surface but are dangerous enough to sink any sale. Unlike the most common objections—about price, for instance—these objections may seem trivial. Buyers may be afraid to voice them because they don't want to appear silly or unreasonable. Or the buyers themselves may dismiss the concerns as silly and not realize that, silly or not, they are still powerful. Finally, these objections are often emotional—and therefore not easily resolved with logic.

Rick has always been really good at dealing with secondary objections. Even when he lost the nerve to deal with the primary objections, he wouldn't let us forget the secondary objections. He thought they were so important that he even got S.P. and Barbie to help him find out what we needed to know.

S.P. was the perfect person to help, because she loves to ask questions. Getting at secondary objections is all about asking questions. Remember, the best offense is a good defense, so the questions should be direct: Do you have any concerns we haven't talked about? Does anything about this sale worry you? If you could change one thing about my product (or service), what would it be? Encourage people to mention things that may not seem important to them. Buzz never thought that how we packed our product was worth mentioning until Connie asked him about it on Customer Appreciation Day.

There Are No Trivial Objections. Any Decision Can Make or Break a Deal.

Invite customers to question you, too. Think about how people order food, whether it's an entrée at a restaurant or an ice cream cone at the corner stand. In their minds, they state their primary objections ("I don't want fish," or "I want something chocolate") and narrow their choices. Then, they often pose questions: "How spicy is this dish?" or "Does that one have nuts in it?" These questions are a way of stating secondary objections. The questions allow people to gather information without appearing too silly ("I won't eat anything that has olives in it.").

These objections are often easily overcome: "The chef can make that less spicy for you." Objections may not be resolved so easily when people are making important decisions. Still, listen to the questions your customers ask—they are flagging their secondary objections for you.

Even if you can't overcome the objection, you will know why your prospect isn't buying. Over time, you may see patterns you can address.

Many Objections Are Easily Overcome.

Many objections that are not so easily overcome are emotional. Most objections are directly related to what's offered—price, features, and so on. In contrast, emotional objections are only indirectly related to the offer. They come from within the customer. Although the emotional response may be triggered in some way by the offer, it isn't really *about* the offer.

For example, as Rick was trying to make some new deals, he ran into emotional objections from two prospects. One prospect resisted any kind of change; the other resisted anything she felt boxed her in and limited her freedom. Both feelings turned out to be substantial obstacles.

Finding these emotional objections isn't easy. The challenge for any salesperson is that most people aren't even aware of their emotional objections or wouldn't identify them as such. Therefore, asking direct questions isn't effective. Instead, these objections are best uncovered indirectly. Ask general questions about the customer's business. Ask about recent successes and challenges. Find out what made them uncomfortable, and look for themes in their comments. (Someone who complains a lot about change in his or her organization isn't likely to embrace any change you offer, either.) Sometimes, getting this information from other people is easier. We don't always see ourselves as clearly as other people do. That's why Rick had Noreen talk to the prospect's assistant: She knew how his emotions ruled his business decisions.

Once you've identified emotional objections, then what? Sometimes there's nothing you can do: You'll never sell parachute jumps to someone terrified of heights. But in many cases, you can help the customer feel more comfortable. With the prospect who fears being boxed in, for example, you can point out how many opportunities she has to change her mind. (Then you can ease your own fear that she'll exercise every one of them by reassuring yourself that the idea of options probably matters more than the reality.) If you can, alter your offer in some way to ease the prospect's concern.

Emotional Objections Are the Most Difficult to Overcome. But You Can Do It.

We all know that objections are inevitable. They aren't inherently a problem. They become a problem when they are our primary focus: We spend more time focusing on overcoming the objections than we do selling the rewards. That's too bad, because we end up accomplishing exactly the opposite of what we intend.

I remember once when Noreen was buying a printer for our division. We had all met and decided which features we needed. We also decided that we didn't need a high-speed printer—that other features were more important. Noreen had two salespeople come in and give us presentations and demos. The first one heard Addison say that we wouldn't really use high-speed printing. He spent the rest of his presentation telling us why we were going to love high-speed printing. He was so insistent about it that even after he left we called him High-Speed Guy.

The other salesperson spent her time showing us all the features that we said were important. When Addison raised the high-speed issue, she just said, "I thought that wasn't a priority for this group." We ended up buying from her. Noreen had a lot of fun with it because it turned out that both salespeople were showing us the same printer.

Don't Draw Undue Attention to the Reasons People Have *Not* to Buy.

Maybe I've done what I've warned you not to do: I've spent a lot of space talking about objections—the reasons people find *not* to buy. Objections can't be ignored. But they aren't the most important consideration, either. If they were, very few people would ever buy anything. People find reasons *to* buy. Stay focused on those reasons.

May 23, 2001

Ms. Miranda Woodley
Senior Vice President, New Business Initiatives
Upp & Cummings, Inc.
5250 Valencia Dr.
Central City, USA 33333

Dear Miranda:

Thank you for taking the time to join Barbie and me for lunch. It was a pleasure to continue discussing the ways in which Global Gadget can support Upp & Cummings' entry into the do-it-yourself market. Your success in that exciting venture can also be our success. Miranda, you know that in choosing Global Gadget you can count on getting quality gadgets every time. Your do-it-yourself customers will immediately recognize that Upp & Cummings' products are a great value. As you enter the new market, you can be confident that you are getting fair pricing and competitive payment terms.

Your plans are exciting, but of course this is uncharted territory for Upp & Cummings. We certainly understand your interest in limiting your financial exposure until the launch is a proven hit with consumers.

Global Gadget can help. You may purchase all the gadgets you need for the initial rollout without signing a long-term contract. Instead, you may simply reorder as sales warrant. Over lunch, you inquired about volume discounts. Global Gadget has always extended volume discounts to our loyal customers. Ordinarily, those discounts are written into our contracts. Given the nature of your initiative, we are happy to offer you an alternative. You can buy the initial order at the price quoted, but when you place a follow-up order (provided you meet our volume discount minimums) we will extend a retroactive discount on the first order. You can also save by prepaying for any order.

You also inquired about options for customizing any gadgets you order. Of course we can customize your order in numerous ways, and you do not need to sign a contract to choose from several options. Miranda, this is an exciting opportunity and we look forward to being part of it. I'll call you Tuesday to answer any questions you may have. Have a great Memorial Day weekend.

Regards,

Rick Newman
Senior Sales Consultant

Figure 12.1 *This sales letter from Rick focuses almost entirely on the prospect's secondary objection—her resistance to getting locked into a contract.*

food for thought

Gray's Notebook

1. *Assume that customers have at least three reasons not to buy your product or service beyond price, features, or terms. How can you get this information?*

2. *Think about the last major purchase you made. What were your secondary objections? Did you state them? If so, did the salesperson address them? If you did not state them, how did you resolve them—or did you? If you did not, did your objections color the sale—did you feel buyer's remorse? What can you learn from how the salesperson handled the situation? What do you wish he or she had done differently?*

3. *Don't get so focused on overcoming objections that you forget the reasons the customer was interested in the first place. Make a list of all the reasons the customer has for buying. If you are selling cars, for example, you might list color, warranty, and safety features. Make sure you repeat those points as often as possible.*

4. *Ask questions to help you understand your customer's emotions about the deal. Is he or she excited, worried, frightened, confused? Underscore the positive emotions and confront the negative ones. Don't just ignore emotions in the hopes they'll go away or won't really matter.*

Addison's Brain Trust

Wait, there's more! Check out these books for additional information and insight:

Secrets of Power Negotiating for Salespeople by Roger Dawson (Career Press, 1999)
24 Sales Traps by Dick Canada (Amacom, 2002)

S.P. Surfs the Internet

How do you handle objections when making a sales call?

- ★ Tune in (acknowledge some): 60%
- ★ Turn on (respond to each one): 34%
- ★ Drop out (what objections?): 6%

Source: WorkingWounded.com/ABCnews.com online ballot

Rick's Smart Talk

"What on earth would man do with himself if something didn't stand in his way?"

—*H.G. Wells*

Connie's Smart Questions

One time I took my kids to get their portraits taken. I explained what I wanted, but then the photographer kept trying different things. Each time I stopped him to tell him how I wanted the pictures to be. Finally he got mad and told me I was whiny. Well, I am *not* a whiner. The truth is that he wasn't really listening to me. If you have a potential customer who keeps whining, maybe they feel you haven't heard them. Ask yourself:

- Have you heard what they're trying to say?
- Have you shown that you understand them?
- Did you see if they have solutions to the problem they're describing?
- Did you bring in other resources to help, rather than just shooting from the hip?
- Did you let them know that you appreciate their time and consideration?
- Will you stay in touch even if you lose the sale?

Gray's Anatomy of Business

One of these days I'm going to ask my real estate agent for a cut of her commission. I think she owes at least four sales to me. That's because I was so impressed with how she helped us when we were buying our house that I told her I would vouch for her. I didn't know how often she would take me up on it! But whenever she has someone on the fence about giving her a listing, she has that person call me. She calls me her secret weapon. You have secret weapons, too, when it comes to dealing with objections: satisfied customers. I know—you don't want to annoy them. But it does make sense to create your own network of customers that you can call on for testimonials and support. Ask some of your best customers if they'd be willing to serve as references.

Barbie's Brainy Glossary

Inside scoop　Crucial information that is only available from someone "inside," or close to the action or source. *Access Hollywood* gets the inside scoop on the stars by talking to their assistants and bodyguards.

Salad fork　The utensil placed at the far left in a standard place setting. It should be used first, to eat the salad course. If there is no salad course, it may be used for dessert.

Secondary objections　Objections that customers usually don't feel are important enough to mention but that may still be enough to kill a sale. These objections are often emotional and sometimes subconscious.

chapter thirteen

Building Relationships

How to Listen, Establish Trust, and Go the Extra Mile for Your Customers

Rick once told me, "People don't buy products and services. They buy other people." He didn't mean literally, of course. He meant that people usually buy when they like and trust the people they are buying from. The more expensive the item, the more true that is.

Think about your own buying habits. You may not care who's behind the counter ringing up a greeting card or CD. But if you're buying a car, will you really spend hours haggling over the deal and contract with someone you don't like? Sometimes we don't have a choice—but if we do, we'll exercise that choice. The opposite is true, too. We're more likely to buy—even things we didn't originally intend to buy—when we trust the relationship.

All of that is especially true in business selling, which thrives on repeat business. Rick's sales guru, Jim Cathcart, goes so far as to say that "business should be practiced as an act of friendship, rather than merely as a process of negotiation." Cathcart uses the phrase *relationship selling*. Among other things, relationship selling includes understanding the customer's needs and situation, telling the truth to build trust, and ensuring that the customer remains satisfied with his or her decision.

Strong Relationships Yield Strong Sales.

Here's an example of understanding the customer's needs and situation. Barbie used to talk all the time about this guy Joe, who worked at one of the shoe stores in the mall. She bought a pair of shoes from him one time because he took the time to help her find a pair that she really liked. She didn't think much about the transaction until she went into the store again a few weeks later. Not only did Joe remember her (and what she bought), but he had set aside several pairs of new arrivals that were similar to what she chose the first time.

Soon Barbie was stopping in every couple of weeks, and Joe always had things set aside for her to look at. Not only was Barbie getting the first shot at new styles, but Joe was saving her a lot of time. She noticed that Joe was helping all his customers that way. Each time she went in, he was helping three or four customers while the other salespeople stood around. Naturally, Barbie sent all her friends to see Joe, too. Unfortunately, after a few months Joe was transferred to another store out of the area. The next time Barbie went in, no one even spoke to her. She hasn't been back since. She still talks about Joe, though. "It was never only about the shoes," she says.

For us at Global Gadget, it shouldn't be only about the gadgets either. You may remember that when Barbie called our contact at Kitchen Cartel, he told her that one of the things he disliked about us is that every time he placed an order it was as if we had never heard of him. Customers want to feel they are building on an existing relationship, not starting over each time they speak to you. They want to feel valued.

Work *with* Your Customers, Don't Just Sell *to* Them.

A relationship with your customer is like any relationship: It takes time to earn their trust and moments to lose it. Customers want the truth, because without it they can't make informed decisions. For example, suppose you go out to dinner and the restaurant you choose has people waiting. When you put your name in, the host will tell you how long the wait is. If the host is doing his job, you'll actually wait less than what you were told. If you're told the wait is 15 minutes and you're still waiting at the 30-minute mark, are you a happy customer? At one level, it's just annoying. In some cases, it could affect other plans: If you miss your movie because you weren't seated for dinner, you *really* aren't a happy customer.

Unfortunately, many salespeople are afraid to tell the truth. They withhold some information, or share partial truths, or just plain lie. They do it in the belief that customers will buy when they hear what they want to hear. It's true that customers want to hear certain things, but *only if they are true.* Let's go back to the restaurant. Suppose the wait isn't 15 minutes—it's 90 minutes. (That has actually happened to us when we've gone to a popular brewery in town on Friday night.) Naturally, Taupe and I have been disappointed to get that news—it isn't what we wanted to hear. Still, we can then decide to stay or not to stay. If we don't stay, we'll be back. But if we were told 30 minutes and it became 90, that would be the last time we ate there. Sooner or later, customers always find out the truth. If the truth is different than what they've been told, you've lost their trust.

Truth is more than accuracy. It includes a willingness to stand behind what you say. In other words, are you willing to put your money where your mouth is? If you're working with someone, part of their expectation is that when something goes wrong you will stand with them. If an order is delayed, for example, how will you help them meet their business commitments? Part of earning their trust is having a backup plan in place should your regular systems fail.

Telling the Truth May Cost You Some Business in the Short Term. But in the Long Run, It Will Pay Off.

If you're pursuing a business relationship for the long term, you can't disappear as soon as the sale is complete. The first time a customer calls with a problem and gets the runaround, the relationship is damaged. Even if you ultimately solve the problem, don't put your customer through hoops first. So many companies respond to a problem only after putting the whole burden on the customer to gather information and manage the process. Don't force your customer to keep calling you. Take the initiative to stay in touch and take responsibility for solving problems.

Sales Don't End. They Are Ongoing.

Maintaining a good customer relationship is tough. It takes time, effort, and often money. But there are many rewards. Customers who trust you will forgive mistakes and problems. But the real reward is the business itself. Remember, replacing a customer costs much more than keeping one. What happened to us is ample proof of that.

relationship selling checklist

____**Prepare to Sell: Build and Sustain Sales Readiness**
Lay a lot of groundwork. Keep numerous prospects in the pipeline. Contact them often. Keep them current on your new products, special deals, and other news.

____**Target the Right Prospects: Identify Who, How, and When to Make Contact**
Work with the person who can really make the decision to buy. Adapt your style to the customer's style—contact them when and how they prefer. Don't let the "maybe" stage last forever. Some prospects will say "no," and it's better if they do so sooner rather than later.

____**Connect with the Person: Establish Truthful Communication, Build Trust**
Be a trusted advisor. Offer helpful information about your product and the market. Anticipate what your customer will want to know and offer the information before he or she has to ask. Always be honest in your communication.

____**Assess the Needs: Understand the Needs of the Person and the Situation**
Work to understand your customer's business as well as your own. Understand the challenges he or she faces and work to solve problems. Understand other issues the customer faces internally; do what you can to help him or her sell the deal.

____**Solve the Main Problem: Cause the Person to Experience the Value You Bring**
Sell the value. For example, if you train employees to understand sexual harassment, the real value to the customer is a more productive, more respectful workplace and fewer complaints and lawsuits.

____**Commit to the Sale: Confirm that a Purchase Has Been Made**
Really close the sale—ask for the business and acknowledge the sale when you get it. Put your commitment in writing. Make sure there are no surprises.

____**Ensure Satisfaction: See that the Customer Remains Satisfied with His or Her Decision**
Don't disappear after you make the sale. Monitor key milestones in the deal (such as the first delivery of product) and contact the customer to make sure that there are no problems.

____**Manage Your Sales Potential: Lead, Motivate, and Grow Yourself**
Set your own targets and work toward them.

Figure 13.1 *While he was working to win new business, Rick did some research on relationship selling. He found a list of sales guru Jim Cathcart's eight competencies of relationship selling. Rick took the original list and annotated it himself for the rest of his sales team.*

food for thought

Gray's Notebook

1. *How much do you really know about your most important customers? Make a list of your 10 most important customers (you define the criteria for "most important"). For each one, you should know their primary products or services, their approximate annual revenue, the key decision makers in the firm, their market position, their approximate market share, their greatest business challenges, their chief competitors, and their key customers. Do you?*

2. *Develop the reputation of someone who tells the truth (even if it means losing an occasional sale).*

3. *The sales process never ends. Keep reselling key customers. Remember, your competitors won't stop selling just because you've landed a deal—they'll try to steal the business away. Keep in touch with customers and stay abreast of what they're being offered. Work with customers—don't just sell to them. Help connect them with other resources.*

4. *Keep on top of everything happening with key customers. Your customers interact with people in other departments (such as customer service or billing) all the time. Other departments can be a great source of information. Also, you don't want to be surprised if a customer asks you about his or her account.*

Addison's Brain Trust

Wait, there's more! Check out these books for additional information and insight:

Everyday Negotiation by Deborah M. Kolb and Judith Williams (Jossey-Bass, 2003)
Smart Moves: 140 Checklists to Bring Out the Best in You and Your Team by Samuel D. Deep, Lyle Sussman, et al. (Addison-Wesley, 1997)

S.P. Surfs the Internet

The old model of selling versus the new model:

★ The old model (pre-1970s): 40% closing, 30% prospecting, 20% qualifying, 10% establishing rapport
★ The new model: 40% building trust, 30% identifying needs, 20% presenting solutions, 10% confirming and closing

Source: Business guru Brian Tracy

Rick's Smart Talk

"Only a fool holds out for top dollar."

—*Joseph Kennedy*

Connie's Smart Questions

I ship a lot of packages to our customers from the warehouse. Most of them get where they are supposed to go with no problems, but some do not. When packages are lost or delayed, I better be able to tell our customer what's happening. When I know packages are really important, I always call to make sure they have arrived. I learned a long time ago that getting packages out on time to the right destination and properly packed is only half the job. The other half is follow-up. Rick says that's true in sales, too. Ask yourself:

- Do you consider follow-up with each customer to be part of the sale?
- Do you follow up with each customer after the sale?
- Do you see follow-up as a free focus group to learn about your customer, your product, or your service?
- Do you address whatever concerns are raised during follow-up?

For two months, keep track of all the issues your customers raise during your follow-up. How many of them could you address up front? Have your customers offered you ideas for improving your product or service?

Gray's Anatomy of Business

Get a piece of paper. Divide it into three columns. In the first column, list each customer's major business objectives. In the second, list obstacles that prevent them from achieving these objectives. In the third column, write your solutions.

Barbie's Brainy Glossary

Relationship selling Looking past making just one sale to develop a relationship in which you can make multiple sales. This means that sometimes you may have to sacrifice one commission (if the customer isn't comfortable) to maintain the relationship.

Trust Reliance on the character, ability, strength, or truth of someone. Like how I know that my sister won't ever tell Mom about some of my dates.

chapter fourteen

Closing the Sale

How to Ask Customers for Their Business

This is the most important thing I learned in college: Sooner or later, you have to turn in the final. It's not that I thought I had a choice, exactly. But I would be working on the exam and get stuck on something, or I would realize that I had made an error earlier and go back to it. Too often, I'd misjudge the time and the professor would call for the test booklets and I wasn't finished. Even though I knew that I didn't know the answers to some questions, I held out hope that until I turned in the test I might figure them out. I learned the hard way how to be smarter.

The same thing happens in sales. Rick was pretty famous throughout the company for taking a sale all the way to the last stage and then dawdling. He found a million reasons to delay asking for the sale. I understand why: If he didn't ask for the sale, no one could say "no." The problem, of course, is that no one could say "yes" either. By the time he did finally ask for the business, often the prospect had said "yes" to somebody else.

Sooner or later you have to bite the bullet and go for the close.

Work Out the Details Before You Ask for the Business.

Imagine a car salesman presenting a contract before you've decided what color or even what model you want. Does that sound crazy? It happens all the time—in car sales and many other businesses. Maybe that sounds like a different problem—asking for the business too soon. Actually, it's the same problem because people can't say "no" to an incomplete offer. Asking too soon, therefore, is a stalling technique. Salespeople hope to get a general agreement and work out the details later. Occasionally that works. More often, the deal falls apart later on details.

The time to close the sale is when you've worked out the details and collected as much information as you can. If you've done your work, by that point you understand what the client needs and how you can help. You've worked through primary and secondary objections. You've told the truth and earned their trust.

By the Time You Ask for the Sale, There Should Be No Surprises.

No matter how many questions you ask, some clients will withhold information and can nix a deal for a reason you've never heard before. Most, however, will be up-front. That doesn't mean that you won't need to negotiate during the final phase of the sale. Your customers' first obligation is to their own businesses, so they will pursue the best deal possible. (Some clients thrive on negotiation, too, and will see how much they can get away with.)

Whatever their motivation, you should give yourself some leeway. Look at the elements of the deal and decide where you can give the buyer price, delivery date, payment terms, billing date . . . something. Wait until you have worked out the framework of the deal before you negotiate where you can. Rick had a habit of tossing bones to prospects before he even had to. For example, the client would ask about payment terms. Rick would say, "30 days," and then without pausing for air add, "but we can stretch that to 60 if need be." Once that was said, 60 days was a done deal—and he had one less negotiating ploy at the end when he needed it.

Before you start the negotiating process, draw your mental line in the sand. Auto dealers are notorious for their negotiating tactics, but you can't negotiate them into a free car.

Allow Some Give and Take, but Know Your Limits.

As part of your close, revisit the emotions you uncovered earlier in the process. What is the customer excited about? How are you making his or her life easier? What's going to be better after he or she says "yes"? Facts are facts, but people don't buy a house based on square footage alone. Emotions play a big part in most purchases, and people are more likely to close themselves if they are feeling good.

Many people will, anyway. Our marketing studies over the years have confirmed earlier studies about consumer behavior. Many people are *pleasure seekers*—that is, they make the decision they think will reward them most. In business sales, the reward might be higher profit, happier customers, or a promotion. An effective line for these people is, "If you do this, then . . ."

More of us are *pain avoiders*. We make the decision that we think will help avoid something negative. In business, that may mean avoiding the boss's wrath, preventing a lawsuit, or hanging onto market share. An effective line for these people is, "Do this or else . . ." Know your clients well enough to know which personality type they have; appeal to that personality.

For both groups, you want to lay the groundwork to avoid buyer's remorse. You don't want the pleasure seekers to feel they're missing out on their reward or the pain avoiders to feel the pain anyway. Set expectations and reinforce why they've gotten this far in the buying process.

Don't Neglect Your Buyer's Emotions When You Ask for the Sale.

Closing a sale, like taking a final, is both science and art. In both cases, the science is in doing your homework and preparing as best you can. The art is in making the best use of your time to score the most points possible. And turning in the final? That's common sense.

training department

Closing the Sale: Role-Play Exercises

We've identified the eight most effective closes here. Working with a partner (or, if required, two partners), role-play each of them. Using the situation outlined, improvise the dialogue to make the sale. At the end of each role play, switch roles and let the person who was the salesperson the first time now play the customer. Incorporate what you learn into your closes.

The Puppy Dog Close
Set up a situation in which the customer can take the product home and live with it. Explore what will happen after the customer gets the product home.

The Don't Settle All the Details up Front Close
The customer is focused on the details of the deal, and you're bogged down. Work to get the prospect to agree in principle to buy, and then negotiate the details. Circle back to the agreement in principle to reinforce to the customer that he or she is getting what he or she wanted.

The Contingency Close
The customer is almost ready to buy—provided an obstacle is removed. Get the prospect to agree to buy if something else happens first (as, for example, when someone makes an offer on a house contingent on their current home selling first).

The Split the Difference Close
Choose a price between your offer and what the customer is willing to pay. Sell him or her on the compromise.

The "That Wouldn't Stop You from Going Ahead Today, Would It?" Close
The prospect raises numerous "Yes, but what if?" scenarios. Put the customer's concerns in context; close him or her by eliminating the reasons not to buy today.

The Divide and Conquer Close
This role play requires two customers. In this situation, both of them have to agree before you get a sale. Sell each separately, and then use each to help convince the other.

The Good Cop/Bad Cop Close
This role play requires two salespeople. One salesperson should try for the hard close while the other sympathizes with the customer but still reiterates the selling points.

The "What Did I Do Wrong?" Close
Get the client to narrow his or her resistance to just one objection—then overcome that objection.

Figure 14.1 *Rick's confidence was so shaky that he had a hard time closing sales. He worked with the training department to develop this role-playing exercise to strengthen closing skills.*

food for thought

Gray's Notebook

1. *What is your bottom line? Before you negotiate, know exactly how much you can give and where. Make a list of every element of the deal you're proposing (e.g., price, payment terms, guarantee, delivery date). For each one, write beside it how much maneuvering room you have—and then stick to it.*
2. *Don't offer concessions until you have to. If you make the deal easier (such as by extending the deadline) before you have to, you'll have less to work with later. Think of yourself as a basketball coach: Don't use up all your time-outs before you get to the final quarter of the game.*
3. *Ask for their business. (Duh! Some salespeople lay all the groundwork but fall short because they never ask for the business.)*
4. *Joe Friday was wrong! You must present the facts, but you also must address the customer's emotional needs and concerns.*
5. *Don't become a stranger; follow up after the sale.*

Addison's Brain Trust

Wait, there's more! Check out these books for additional information and insight:

Getting to Yes by Roger Fisher, William Ury, and Bruce Patton (Penguin, 1991)
Zig Ziglar's Secrets of Closing the Sale by Zig Ziglar (Berkeley, 1985)

S.P. Surfs the Internet

What is most important to a customer? Here's how salespeople and customers respond:

★ Building trust: 17% of customers agree, 28% of salespeople agree
★ Building relationships: 14% of customers agree, 15% of salespeople agree
★ Selling value: 12% of customers agree, 20% of salespeople agree
★ Problem solving: 9% of customers agree, 13% of salespeople agree
★ Adding value: 8% of customers agree, 3% of salespeople agree

Source: Selling 2.0 *by Josh Gordon (Berkeley, 2000)*

Rick's Smart Talk

"A bashful beggar has an empty purse."

—*Hungarian proverb*

Connie's Smart Questions

In a wedding, there is only one way to seal the deal: with "I do." But there are many options for sealing any other kind of deal. In fact, Rick says there are as many closes as there are different types of customers. Here are a few examples:

- Do you offer incentives?
- Do you apply time pressure?
- Do you enlist their support?
- Do you offer a guarantee?
- Do you help your customers sell to their boss, coworkers, and others?
- Do you minimize their concerns? For example, do you give them a test drive or a period in which to use the product with no risk?

Track your closings for 90 days. Try different approaches and see which works best. Is there a pattern of which type of close works with which type of customer?

Gray's Anatomy of Business

Have you ever noticed how you can convince someone of something and that what closed the deal wasn't what you thought it was? It happens all the time. So don't rely on your intuition: Do an autopsy on successful sales pitches to see what clinched the deal. Collect this data and incorporate it into future sales pitches.

Barbie's Brainy Glossary

Consultative sales   An approach in which you focus on solving your customer's problems instead of on your own commission. Like when Joe used to send me to another shoe store because he didn't have what I needed.

Hard close   A technique in which you put a lot of pressure on the customer to buy. It usually only works when the customer has few options.

Soft close   A low-pressure close.

part 3

THE SEVEN DEADLY WORKPLACE SINS

chapter fifteen

Exhaustion

How to Set Priorities, Say "No," and Ease Your Stress

If a genie ever grants me three wishes, one of them is going to be for every human to have a reboot button. That way, when we get overwhelmed, someone can just push the button and restart us. Is it really such a crazy idea? It works for computers.

I've really mastered rebooting my computer. That's because it either freezes or crashes or freezes and then crashes at least once a day. I'll be working away and then suddenly I'm just moving my mouse around the pad for exercise. Hasn't that happened to you? S.P. tells me that it happens because I'm asking the computer to do too many things at once. She tells me that the computer only has so much active memory, and when that memory maxes out the system fails.

I'm not impressed. Computer nerds like S.P. are always telling us that computers are better than we are—that they are faster, can process more data, and so on. I say phooey. If I want to use something that will freeze and crash when it tries to do too much, I'll use my brain. My brain gets overwhelmed regularly, and when that happens the symptoms are all too CPU: My head recycles the same material in an endless loop, my eyeballs (read: monitor) glaze over, and I crash.

Our brains may as well have been networked after Virginia dropped her double bombshell of less time and more work. It seemed we all had system failure. As I walked around the office, everyone seemed dazed. But total system failure was a luxury we could not afford.

All of Us Can Only Process Just So Much.

A luxury? Yes, because our meltdowns were little more than a way of wallowing in our fatigue. It may feel good to walk around like a zombie and ask people to feel sorry for you. But nothing is getting done while you're being a zombie, and the only way to get out from underneath feeling overwhelmed is to get things done.

But how do we get things done when we feel so overwhelmed? We have to turn around and face the witch. Replay *The Wizard of Oz* in your head. Dorothy was pretty overwhelmed toward the end of the film. Ultimately, she had to stop running, face the witch, and melt her.

A variation on the same plan works for us. The first thing to do is stop running. It's true that very few of us literally run from the workload and bolt from the building. But we do run for help, hoping that someone (probably the boss) will make it better. Or we procrastinate. Or we allow a small setback to derail us. (One afternoon our computer network was down for a couple of hours, and everyone spent the entire time complaining that they couldn't work. I'm pretty confident that people worked without computers for thousands of years, actually.)

Confront the Stress Directly.

It would be nice if we could just find a bucket of water and melt the workload. But we can't, so we have to do the next best things. The first is to recognize that there is a lot of pressure in the workplace to make *everything* urgent. It happens in part because some people are afraid that their projects will end up on the back burner and seem unimportant—and so, by extension, will they. It also happens because people procrastinate or can't get to a project for a while, so that it becomes urgent because time is running out. It happens because some people thrive on crises.

Whatever the reasons, we can't let everything stay urgent. Take the time to revisit all the work and establish some priorities. When you do that, don't let the first thing that's due be the one that always gets to the top of the list. Instead, think about the project that will have the greatest impact on profit or customer satisfaction. The extra work the CEO dumped on us was making us crazy precisely because it was irrelevant to our real priority: saving the division.

But the CEO is the CEO, so we couldn't just ignore the assignment. We also couldn't let the DVD gadget replace important work. So we let it replace other irrelevant work. There's a fair amount of that in every workplace. Noreen found so many pointless tasks that it made her giddy: changes to changes to changes on some of our forms, distributing meeting agendas to people who weren't even invited to attend, and on and on. We have to defend our time as if it were gold—because it is.

Identify Tasks that Don't Add Value—and Stop Doing Them.

After we've eliminated the tasks that add no value, we need to look at the remaining tasks and figure out how they add value. I plead guilty to ignoring that advice for far too long. I was the worst in the division at devoting far too much energy and time to the wrong tasks.

I'm a perfectionist at heart, so I always wanted every job I touched to be done perfectly. In theory, that sounds like a great way to sustain quality. In reality, it's just lazy. For example, every drawing I did was done with the same care. That meant that a product drawing that was going to be used to tune our production machinery and create a prototype got the same attention as a product drawing so that Sherman could create the packaging. I'm embarrassed to say that it never occurred to me that Sherman needed a lot less information to do his work.

In the same way, Noreen took just as much time proofing and formatting internal memos as customer proposals. And Addison spent as much time auditing the donut fund as the travel budget. Understand, I'm not advocating sloppiness. I'm advocating working smarter.

Identify the Appropriate Quality Standard for Each Task and Then Work to Meet That Standard.

We live and work in stressful times. Some stress (maybe even a lot of stress) is inevitable, and these techniques won't eliminate it all. But stress should not be so overwhelming that we stop functioning. When that happens to you, these techniques can help. Think of them as your reboot button. They helped get us back on track.

not-to-do list

We all have to-do lists. But these lists can be filled with tasks that rob us of the time we need to do the most important work. Make a list of the things you don't have to do—or even shouldn't be doing. It's easy to pick silly things (such as drafting and circulating a memo on the proper ways to use the recycling bins), but it's tougher to identify ongoing parts of your job that are extraneous or redundant. Force yourself to choose some things and list them here. Then don't do them!

1. _____
2. _____
3. _____
4. _____
5. _____
6. _____
7. _____
8. _____
9. _____
10. _____

Figure 15.1 *After our original six-month time frame was cut, we knew we had to make changes or we'd never succeed in turning the division around. We all agreed we had to cut out everything we didn't absolutely have to do. We all drafted not-to-do lists and posted them in our cubicles. If we slipped and did something on the list, we fined ourselves $5. At the end of the project we used that money to throw ourselves a nice party—not a potluck.*

food for thought

Gray's Notebook

1. Make "no" a part of your workplace vocabulary. Accept that you can't do everything, and don't agree to more than you can reasonably do. Saying "yes" at the outset may feel like the right thing to do politically, but if you can't deliver you'll suffer politically.

2. Negotiate deadlines and projects. Things happen that create more and unexpected work. When that happens, take a look at the projects already on your plate. Which ones can you delay, cancel, or get help with? Don't assume your boss remembers everything you're working on; remind him or her.

3. Forget trying to be perfect; identify the minimum quality standard that each project requires. Some things need to be letter-perfect; many do not. Invest your time where it matters most.

4. Question priorities. Not everything is a crisis or demands top priority. Don't let other people make *their* priorities *your* priorities. Focus on the top priorities for the business and for your customers. Defend your time—remind your coworkers that your time matters, too. Show respect for them by not intruding on their priorities.

Addison's Brain Trust

Wait, there's more! Check out these books for additional information and insight:

A Simpler Way by Margaret J. Wheatley and Myron Kellner-Rogers (Berrett-Koehler, 1996)

Smart Moves: 140 Checklists to Bring Out the Best in You and Your Team by Samuel D. Deep, Lyle Sussman, et al. (Addison-Wesley, 1997)

S.P. Surfs the Internet

Which song title sums up the amount of information at work?

★ "I Can't Be Satisfied": 14%
★ "I Can't Remember": 39%
★ "I Can't Find the Time": 47%

Source: WorkingWounded.com/ABCnews.com online ballot

Rick's Smart Talk

"For fast-acting relief, try slowing down."

—*Lily Tomlin*

Connie's Smart Questions

Do I get overwhelmed? I have a husband, three kids, a crazy mother-in-law, an unemployed brother, two goldfish, a full-time job, a lazy boss, and a demanding English teacher. What do you think? When it gets to be too much, take stock. Ask yourself these questions:

- Are you organizing your time so you focus on the most important stuff?
- What is your peak performance time? I'm a morning person, so I always try to tackle my most important project then. Do you schedule your time so you work on the most important stuff when you are at your best?
- Do you celebrate each victory?
- Do you delegate what you can to other people?
- Are you getting enough rest, appropriate nutrition, and exercise?
- Do you take breaks and use your lunch hour so you can get some time away from work?
- Do you try to leave your work at work and not take it home with you?

Maybe you are too overwhelmed to do all that! Commit to doing just one of those things each week. Write down what you are going to do and post it. Follow through on that one thing all week. After you've done them all, keep using the ones that worked best for you.

Gray's Anatomy of Business

I remember one day I had two tasks that had to be done: (1) a regular report for Addison that had to be filled out in triplicate and (2) updating Virginia on our efforts to reinvent the division. Did I do them both with the same level of energy? Of course not. I gave the report the minimum effort (about 60 percent) so I could spend more time on the important stuff. Look at the projects on your desk. What is the minimum quality standard that you need to apply to each? And what is the really important stuff that deserves your full attention? Make a list of every project you have, and beside each one indicate the minimum attention it needs.

Barbie's Brainy Glossary

Perfectionist   One who regards anything less than perfect as unacceptable.

Sheep   A timid person who is easily led. Like all those people who wear pants that are much too big and fall down around their knees.

Stressed out   Suffering from unbearably high levels of mental tension, usually resulting from too much to do or too many pressures.

chapter sixteen

Anger

How to Keep Things in Perspective and Manage Your Emotions

Here's what I really want in my morning news: a road rage forecast. There are some days when every commuter behind the wheel seems to have lost his or her mind. Those are the mornings when drivers speed up to block you when you signal a lane change, when people lean on their horns and shake their fists at other drivers, and when people don't *press* the pedals in their cars—they *stomp* them.

I always arrive at work those mornings a nervous wreck. I feel like I've done battle before I even get to work. No wonder—all that road rage is dangerous. People don't seem to remember there are lives at stake. It's so much craziness over stuff we can't control anyway.

As long as I'm asking for a road rage forecast, I'd like a cubicle rage forecast, too. I'm sure you've seen cubicle rage; it's a lot like road rage. People pull up and try to block your moves; they just do it in meetings instead of in the middle lane. People shake their fists and curse at their fellow employees. People don't *tap* the keys on their keyboards, they *pound* them.

Anger is almost as dangerous in the workplace as it is on the road. It can be lethal to careers, to morale, and to teamwork. Yet, despite the risks, anger is an epidemic in today's workplace.

Anger Is an Acid that Corrodes the Foundations of Any Workplace.

Why is everyone so angry? Usually not for the reasons they say they are angry. People blow off steam over a lot of penny-ante stuff: misunderstandings, false assumptions, surprises, poor communication, missed connections. We've certainly had our fair share of squabbles. Noreen regularly pitches a fit about the food left to spoil in the break room refrigerator. Addison gets snitty about sloppy expense reports. Connie loses her cool when the warehouse guys whine; one day she stuck a pacifier in a guy's mouth.

When Taupe and I fight about the toothpaste cap, it's never really about the toothpaste cap. It's the same at work. The real issues—respect, trust, and fear—stay beneath the surface.

I suppose it doesn't show much respect to give a grown man a pacifier. Connie was having a bad day (once in a while, we all lose it), and she laughs at herself about it now. In any case, careless indignities like that don't eat away at us as much as ongoing indifference to our whole selves.

I've sure seen that watching Taupe. Her job demands a lot of travel, and it has for a long time. Mostly, she's made her peace with the travel. She has learned to maneuver through all the draconian airline policies, and she could teach packing on cable TV. Once she met Mavis, she even managed to keep everything at home running smoothly when she's gone. What really galls her, though, is how cavalier her boss is about the travel. He's forever springing trips on her at the last moment, or adding days to the trip after she's made her plans. He doesn't seem to recognize in any way that Taupe has a life outside work. He never considers how many school events she misses, how many evenings she has to rearrange, how many appointments she has to reschedule. Taupe isn't shy, so she's discussed all this with him several times. He promises to be better, and he is—for about three days.

Every trip seems to make her angrier, and she stays angry longer. I see it spilling over into our lives more and more. Sooner or later, something's going to pop. Either the boss will leave or Taupe will. She loves her job, generally, but she resents how she's treated. If her boss loses her it will really be a stupid blunder on his part because the problem would be so easy to fix.

I kept thinking about Taupe when I was looking around our office. People want to feel that their time, their ideas, their priorities, and their contributions are respected. I also saw that people want to see respect for other people. The team believed that Rick had betrayed S.P. and they turned on him. People underestimate the solidarity of most teams.

Disrespect Breeds Anger that Gets in the Way of the Work.

People reacted so strongly to Rick's apparent betrayal of S.P. because it violated their trust. Trust is crucial in any effective team. Imagine being an airline pilot who didn't trust the copilot, a surgeon who didn't trust the nurses, or a soldier who didn't trust the rest of the unit. Without trust, those people could never be fully effective on the job.

We lose sight of how important trust is in most other jobs. But trust is the glue that holds us together. No wonder we get angry when that trust is violated: Our jobs get a lot harder. Think about the surgeon. If she trusts the nurses, she can focus 100 percent of her energy and attention on the patient. If she doesn't trust the nurses, some part of her has to watch them to make sure they are doing what needs to be done. She's now working hard on two fronts, and none of us wants that.

Distrust weakens any team, and the team members know that. They respond, therefore, by isolating the person responsible and forcing him or her—literally or figuratively—off the team. That's basically what people did to Rick. I felt for him, actually. I experienced that myself when Rick felt I had betrayed him. I became invisible to him, remember? It was a horrible feeling. The punishment for violating someone's trust is harsh, but I understand it.

Of course, that punishment has consequences for the whole team. Communication suffers; workflow is disrupted; ideas are stifled.

Distrust Triggers Many Other Problems.

People also turned on Rick because they were afraid. Juan saw that right away. I wish I had been that smart. But when Juan explained it, I sure got it. At some level, they worried that the distrust they felt would undermine our work. They worried that ultimately we would fail in our efforts to turn the division around, and they would lose their jobs.

So the incident with S.P. stopped being about S.P., and it unleashed a lot of repressed anger. People were angry at Global Gadget about the reorganization, angry with Virginia for how she was handling it, and angry at each other for not doing more to improve things. They were angry about feeling powerless to really do anything.

Fear is a powerful emotion, and it sparks an almost primal response. That's what road rage is largely about: "You could have killed me!" We are afraid. Of course, the way people express their anger on the road does nothing to improve things. The way they express anger at work rarely helps either.

The only thing that does help is dealing with the root issues. Unfortunately, that's usually the last thing we do. Instead, we tinker with the symptoms of the problem. We deal with road rage by advising people about how to reduce their stress instead of developing other transportation options so that there *is* no stress. At work, we vow to take our food out of the refrigerator, do our expense reports properly, and stop whining. We'd be better off finding ways to foster respect, trust, and security.

Subj: Re: In Trouble
Date: 6/13/01 7:48:14 AM Central Daylight Time
From: NStMary@globalgadget.com
To: SPChang
CC GBlanderson, RNewman, JDelToro, SFox, AApplebaum, CSanchez, BFalwell

S.P.—

I *knew* there was something bothering you. It was all over your face this morning. Are you free for lunch? I want all the details of what happened.

That Rick! It's always about him, isn't it? I don't know what he did to betray you, but I'm sure there was no good reason for it. Did he think you wouldn't find out? Well, if he did he was sure wrong.

We'll fix him. I've already talked to Addison and Barbie this morning. Believe me, none of us are talking to him any more. He needs to know that we are a team around here and he better learn to treat everyone well. So far all he cares about is himself and his own career.

I'm so angry I can hardly see straight. It's not bad enough that management has shortened our time AND added extra work, but now we have to watch our backs, too. I don't see how you can be so calm about it.

So lunch . . . when?!

N

Figure 16.1 *This is a good example of an e-mail gone wrong. Noreen noticed that S.P. seemed down the morning they all found out about our new challenges. She sent S.P. an e-mail asking what was up; S.P. responded just by saying she had some concerns about something Rick did. Noreen was already angry about the changes, and the incident with S.P. was the last straw. She fired this back to S.P.—and was so angry she didn't notice that she added her entire department distribution list to it. The e-mail created quite a stir all over the office—it took Noreen months to get past it. It was a good lesson that every e-mail is a historical document, there forever. It was also a good lesson never to write any business document in the heat of the moment.*

LATER, S.P. RETURNS FROM MEETING VIRGINIA.
It's OK. I'm staying.
It turns out it wasn't Rick after all...
...someone from Upp & Cummings ran into Virginia at some seminar.
I explained everything. She said she understood. But what a mess.
You still need to apologize to Rick, you know.
I know.
But that's the least of my problems...
LAYOFFS are coming, Daddy-O...
...And Virginia says that if I'm not leaving, then someone else on our team is going to be let go.

food for thought

Gray's Notebook

1. *Be aware of your emotional state. Few of us are really capable of leaving our emotions at the door when we walk into work. We can manage those emotions if we are aware of them. Each morning, at the start of work, reflect on how you're feeling. If you're angry or upset about something that happened at home, think about how you'll manage those feelings. For example, you might let people know that you are upset about something outside work and ask for their understanding. Keep in mind that emotions are complex and sometimes deceive us. We may feel anger when we actually are afraid—one emotion masks another. If you express an emotion and don't feel an emotional release, you probably have additional—and unexplored—emotions.*
2. *Keep things in perspective. Focus on the long term.*
3. *Find positive addictions (hobbies, exercise, and so on).*
4. *Before you express your anger, ask yourself whether the situation is a battle worth fighting. If we fought about everything that annoyed us, none of us would get any work done. Choose to fight for your point of view when something happens that is counter to your values or threatens a project the organization supports.*

Addison's Brain Trust

Wait, there's more! Check out these books for additional information and insight:

The Courageous Messenger: How to Successfully Speak Up at Work by Kathleen D. Ryan, Dan Oestreich, and George Orr (Jossey-Bass, 1996)

The EQ Edge: Emotional Intelligence and Your Success by Steven J. Stein and Howard E. Book (Stoddart, 2000)

S.P. Surfs the Internet

Great Lies of Management:

* ★ "Employees are our most valuable asset."
* ★ "I have an open-door policy."
* ★ "You could earn more money under the new plan."
* ★ "We're reorganizing to better serve our customers."
* ★ "The future is bright."

Source: The Dilbert Principle *by Scott Adams (HarperCollins, 1996)*

Rick's Smart Talk

"Anger is just one letter short of danger."   —*Anonymous*

Connie's Smart Questions

Many of the guys who work in the warehouse with me are so whiny. They are always unhappy, and they blame everyone and everything for their problems—everyone, that is, except themselves. It drives me crazy, and frankly I don't understand it. I can't imagine giving anyone else that much power over me. I'm responsible for me. Are you? Ask yourself these questions:

- Do you blame everything that happens to you on other people?
- What role do your own actions play in the problems you face?
- Could things change (for the better) if you acted differently?
- Is there anyone who can help you address these issues differently?
- Has your anger gotten you in trouble before?
- Can you respond in a healthier way when bad stuff happens to you?
- Do you know how to make yourself relax?
- Can you change your view of a bad situation?

For the next 30 days, take a few minutes each day to write down incidents that make you angry at work. Pay attention to what triggers your anger. Is there a pattern? Is there anything you could do to avoid getting in that situation? For example, suppose you get angry when you are challenged in a meeting. Maybe you could talk with some people before the meeting to let them know what you're going to say and work through any disagreements in advance.

Gray's Anatomy of Business

I once read an interview with baseball manager Joe Torre. He said that he never got too worked up over what his players were saying, but focused on *why* they were saying it. The same applies to each of us at work. Every time I start feeling angry, I don't get hung up on feeling angry—I try to find the source of the anger. How do I know I'm angry? (Don't laugh—many of us discover far too late.) What causes it? What can I do to mitigate some of the strong emotions?

Barbie's Brainy Glossary

Anger   An intense feeling of displeasure with a person or situation.

Ownership   A willingness to accept feelings as one's own.

Prozac   Happy pills. No more anger.

chapter seventeen

Surrender

How to Leverage Your Influence and Make a Difference

I finally found the source of kryptonite in our office. For a long time I couldn't figure out why we were no longer faster than a DSL connection, more powerful than a CEO's edict, or able to leap tall piles of paperwork in a single bound. We seemed sapped of all our strength, powerless in the face of everything going on around us. Then one day Virginia threw a chunk of kryptonite at my head and knocked some sense into me.

All right, so we never really had super powers and there was no kryptonite. But we were feeling powerless and drained of the life force. And Virginia did wake me up by helping me see that unless you really are Superman, power is pretty illusory.

In my head, our CEO, Mr. Wadsworth, was Superman without the cape and tights. I figured he could do pretty much anything he wanted. He was the one who decided to reorganize the company and upend all our lives. *That's* power. But Virginia reminded me that Wadsworth had to answer to the board of directors, the shareholders, and the Wall Street analysts. She said that everybody has to answer to someone, and I think she was right.

I had confused power with authority. Power is the ability to take action without restraint. Authority is the ability to make decisions and effect change within specific parameters. Put that way, I could see that Wadsworth didn't really have power at all. I mean, he couldn't come into work one day and just decide that we were going to stop making gadgets and make pasta sauce instead.

Power and Authority Are Not the Same Thing. In the Workplace, No One Really Has Power.

So if no one really has power, why do we all feel power*less?* Why do we feel helpless in the face of change, helpless to stop the speeding train from reaching a destination we know is wrong, helpless to control the outcome?

I think it's the same reason we so often feel powerless to lose weight, get in shape, stop smoking, or pay off our credit card debt. Because we are powerless to do any of those things with a snap of our fingers, we feel we can't do them at all. But we *can* lose weight, get in shape, stop smoking, and pay off our credit card debt. It just takes hard work. In short, we're lazy and we want an easy answer.

We're lazy at work, too. Power is the easy answer. Consider the other options. Authority gives us limited control, but it comes tethered to responsibility. Suppose you were suddenly granted authority over scheduling work shifts in your company. No matter where they work, everyone I know thinks that the person in charge of scheduling is an idiot—so here's your chance. Now you can clean up the mess and set up a sensible schedule. Of course, as you do it you have to make sure that all the work gets done on time. You have to meet budget (no unauthorized overtime), honor vacation requests, and respond to unscheduled absences. Authority is no fun, is it?

No One Has Power without Also Having Responsibility.

We don't all want responsibility (if we did, voter turnout would be a lot higher), and even if we did, not everyone can have authority. But there is something that everyone can have, and that's influence. There is an essentially limitless supply of influence. It's cheap, and anybody can have it. So why don't we use our influence more often? Because it's even more demanding than responsibility.

But it's also more effective than power. Once in the sink and think I found this quote from the historian A.J.P. Taylor: "He aspired to power instead of influence, and as a result forfeited both." Influence is so potent because it shapes minds instead of actions. But it isn't as flashy as power (or even responsibility), and it's indirect almost to the point of being invisible. That makes it hard to wield influence.

It is, nonetheless, quite effective. Here's what I realized after Virginia got me thinking about power in new ways: At the midpoint of our project to reinvent the division, the person with the greatest influence was Mavis! Yes, Mavis. Mavis doesn't even work at Global Gadget, and she never met most of the team until later. She has absolutely no power. But she was driving a lot of the project all the same.

Mavis was influencing me, and in turn I was influencing the rest of the team. The funny thing is that Mavis had no designs on influencing or controlling anything. She was just trying to be a good friend to me. She became influential just by being herself. Imagine what she could have accomplished if she had tried to influence things.

Ultimately, Influence Is More Important than Power.

So how did Mavis become so influential? I thought about why I listen to her so much. True, she seems to have known *everyone*. But so has Geraldo Rivera, and I don't listen to him. No, it's more personal than that. First, Mavis is always upbeat but she's also direct. She has a way of being honest and at the same time making you feel good about what she's saying. She suggests things, she doesn't give orders. Sometimes she's so clever in the way she suggests things that I don't even realize what she's doing until later.

You don't have to guess what she's thinking—she just says it straight out. Because she doesn't have an agenda, I trust her. Even though what she says seems so spontaneous, I think she's thought it through pretty carefully. She's always armed with examples, and she puts things in context. She's always aware of the politics of the situation, too. Mavis is a good role model. She radiates happiness and confidence, so you want to be like her.

But mostly, Mavis is great because she never forgets that we're all in this together. She knows we all learn from each other. We all have something to teach and something we need to know. She has a flair for connecting the right idea to the right situation. She's influential because whatever she suggests is ultimately good for everyone.

Connie has a lot of those same qualities, which is why I think she has such influence in the warehouse. She's not the boss out there, you know. It just seems that she is because everyone looks to her.

I'm learning from Connie and Mavis. I learned from Virginia, too. I learned that the kryptonite isn't hidden in the walls or under the floor. The kryptonite is inside us. It's our willingness to surrender our own powers (not our *power*, our *powers*) of responsibility and influence. Me, I'm going to keep trying to leap tall piles of paperwork in a single bound.

w h i n e r s   a n o n y m o u s   c h a p t e r

The 12 Steps To Recovery

1. We admitted we were powerless over our whining—that our lives had become unmanageable.
2. Came to believe that a Higher Power of our understanding could restore us to sanity.
3. Made a decision to turn our will and our lives over to the care of our Higher Power, to help us stop whining and focus on the ways in which we have power or influence.
4. Made a searching and fearless personal inventory of our whining and belief that we are powerless, and recognized the ways in which we did have power and influence.
5. Admitted to our Higher Power, to ourselves, and to another human being the exact nature of our whining and of our assets and influence.
6. Were entirely ready to have our Higher Power remove all temptation to whine or to deny our influence and power.
7. Humbly asked our Higher Power to remove our temptation to whine and to help us to be more positive and to exercise our influence.
8. Made a list of all persons we had harmed with our whining and all projects we had damaged. Became willing to make amends to all those people.
9. Made direct amends to such people wherever possible, except when to do so would injure them or others.
10. Continued to take a personal inventory and when wrong promptly admitted it, while continuing to recognize our progress in valuing our influence and stopping our whining.
11. Sought through prayer and meditation to improve our conscious contact with our Higher Power, praying only for knowledge of our Higher Power's will for us and the power to carry that out.
12. Having had a spiritual awakening as a result of these Steps, we tried to carry this message to other whiners and to practice these principles in all our workplace affairs.

Figure 17.1 *Connie has no patience with whining, and she let us know it. She pointed out how much time we were spending complaining—acting as if we had no power—instead of doing. We all agreed to break the habit. Addison brought in the 12 Steps of Alcoholics Anonymous and adapted them for us. We review these at staff meetings; he says the principles are sound, and the time we spend discussing our habit reminds us how destructive it can be.*

food for thought

Gray's Notebook

1. *Don't get distracted by things beyond your control. There are some ways in which you are powerless. Accept that, and don't spend time trying to change it.*

2. *Identify the places where you have influence. Influence comes from many sources: expertise, knowledge (especially of the past), resources, and personality. Make a list of all the ways in which you can influence situations: Do you have expertise no one else has? Do you control access to information or equipment? Are you well liked? Do you have records from the past that can be helpful?*

3. *Leverage the influence you have. Refer to your list when you're feeling powerless. Ask yourself which of the ways you are influential can be helpful. For example, if you have specialized expertise, prepare a report or presentation that shares your expertise and makes it easy for others to understand.*

4. *Celebrate your successes. Part of why we feel powerless is that we lose track of how much we accomplish and how much change we drive. Make a point of celebrating what you accomplish in some way. Share your successes with others.*

Addison's Brain Trust

Wait, there's more! Check out these books for additional information and insight:

> *Courageous Follower* by Ira Chaleff (Berrett-Koehler, 2003)
> *The End of Bureaucracy and the Rise of the Intelligent Organization* by Gifford Pinchot and Elizabeth Pinchot (Berrett-Koehler, 1993)

S.P. Surfs the Internet

Top reasons that employees decide to leave their jobs:

- ★ Don't know: 4%
- ★ Bored: 5%
- ★ Unhappy with management: 10%
- ★ Lack of recognition: 25%
- ★ Limited chances to advance: 41%

Source: Robert Half International

Rick's Smart Talk

"We too have weapons." —*Franz Kafka*

Connie's Smart Questions

There's nothing like moving to another country to convince you that you have power. You can see that you have the ability to change everything about your life. But even if we don't do anything as dramatic as emigrate, we all have power. We might not be able to snap our fingers and make people jump, but we shouldn't overlook the places where we do have power. Which of these powers will you choose?

- The power of knowledge
- The power to choose how you react
- The power to set standards that influence others
- The power to choose how you'll communicate
- The power of relationships
- The power to speak the truth
- The power of purpose
- The power to learn, grow, and change
- The power to try doing things someone else's way
- The power to resign

For each situation you face at work, write down at least five choices you can make. Which choices will get you furthest? Why?

Gray's Anatomy of Business

If I have one gripe with the people I work with, it's that they think the only way you can get around Global Gadget is on a few big highways. Not true. Any organization is full of back roads. There are usually a million ways to get from point A to point B. Sure, some require that you cover more ground, but they might actually be faster in the long run. Think of a situation you face that feels as if you only have one path that you can follow. Now take a hard look to see if there are other avenues you can pursue (such as finding a new sponsor or working with another department).

Barbie's Brainy Glossary

Empowered   Given the official authority to take action or make a decision.

Jackass: The Movie   Irrefutable proof that the end of Western civilization is near.

Leverage   Deploying a resource to gain advantage. We had more leverage as a team than we did as individuals.

chapter eighteen

Obsolescence

How to Hone Your Skills and Stay on Top of Your Field

Sometimes I think administrative assistants should have to be licensed. Techies, janitors, and human resources people, too. All of us, really. It's not that I'm eager to extend the bureaucracy of testing and review boards. I just think there's something to be said for a system that forces you to keep your job skills current.

Pilots, doctors, beauticians, and others have no choice but to stay current. If they don't, they can't work. The rest of us—unless we have a boss who really promotes our development—are on our own. Unfortunately, that often means that we let our skills wither.

Keeping current is hard. It's expensive. We have too many other things to do. I actually said once, "I'm too busy to learn." Ouch. That's the same thing as saying, "I don't care about my career. It's not worth investing in." It *is* an investment. In that sense, skills are a lot like money. It's tough to think about the money or skills we'll need tomorrow because we're so busy keeping up with today. Unfortunately, tomorrow is almost here.

Our Future Is at Risk Unless We Invest in Our Skills.

We all started thinking about our skills again after Sherman was laid off. It's hard not to when you're imagining a job hunt. I think it was especially hard on Noreen. She's been doing her job a long time, and doing it well. I don't think it occurred to her to focus on learning new software or anything until she imagined herself being compared to others.

The truth is, any of us could have been laid off—or could be laid off tomorrow. When that happens, experience will count for a lot. But so will skills. As you think about what skills you might need, be honest with yourself. I remember when we were interviewing graphics people before Sherman came to work with us. One guy had a lot of experience and a portfolio that we really liked. His designs were really striking, and it was obvious that he "got" package design and product inserts. But during the interview we found out that he hadn't kept up with his computer skills. He didn't know any of the programs we were using, and he had never worked with printers that used electronic files. As much as we liked him, we couldn't hire him. We saw that bringing him up to speed was going to take too much time and be too costly.

Of course, you can get lost on your career path long before you think about a job change. Without current skills, you can be overlooked for promotions or for choice assignments. Even your day-to-day interaction can be affected. Picture the person who is usually the center of attention in your office. Odds are that it's someone seen as highly skilled—the person everyone goes to for help with computer glitches or to have their documents proofread. Honing your skills increases the odds that you'll be in the middle of things, and therefore privy to more information—and more opportunities. The flip side is that the person with out-of-date skills may feel a bit like the kid who is picked last when teams are chosen.

Protect Your Reputation. Don't Be the Person Whose Skills Are Lacking.

So how do those people who are the center of attention stay so sharp? Do they have less to do than the rest of us? Are they just smarter? Or does the boss like them better and send them to more training classes? No, no, and no. They stay sharp because they make it a priority. They also find ways to learn that don't bring their other work to a halt.

For example, all the help they're offering others may not be entirely altruistic. Teaching others turns out to be a great way to learn. One of these days, observe the experts in your office. Pay close attention. In our office, S.P. is the computer guru. But one day I overheard Barbie ask S.P. a question about PowerPoint. I was amazed when S.P. didn't know the answer. So I eavesdropped some more, and as the day went on I realized that S.P. didn't know the answer about half the time. So why do we think she's so smart? I noticed that whenever S.P. didn't know, she took the time to figure it out. She always got it eventually.

I asked S.P. about it later. She said she sees the questions as a good opportunity to learn. For one thing, she's doing something real as opposed to a training exercise. She also said that for her it's easier to learn a few functions at a time than to try to learn a whole program all at once. (I'm not sure that part would work for me, but I understand what she means.) She also said that even if she knows the answer, she doesn't mind helping because it reinforces her own learning.

I don't think S.P. is unique. I've been watching other experts since then, and they are almost always the ones who take the time to learn as they go. S.P.'s method is to figure things out. Some people stay current by actually reading the newspapers and magazines that the rest of us intend to get to "someday." Others surf the Internet and intranets. Some volunteer for committees or special projects they know will let them do something outside their regular job duties. And others find opportunities to learn by practicing their hobbies. For example, Addison volunteered to do his stamp club newsletter so he could learn some graphics software.

Find Ways to Integrate Learning into What You're Already Doing.

All these suggestions involve some self-discipline. If you need structure to help you learn, look around at what your company offers. Enroll in training courses (our training director says there are almost always slots open in our training sessions), or lobby to attend a trade show. Sign up for a community college class. It doesn't really matter how you learn; find a way that works for you. But take it from me: Learning first aid after the bleeding has started is not the best option.

skills maintenance log

Auto warranties are now often five years or 50,000 miles. Even so, cars need to be maintained. They need oil changes, tune-ups, wheel alignments, and so on or they develop problems. The same is true of careers—they need maintenance or they will break down. Use this log to keep track of the maintenance you do on your career.

COMMUNICATION SKILLS
Business Writing, Public Speaking, Graphics, Presentations

List two communication skills that you need in your current job:

1. _____
2. _____

List one communication skill to improve to better position you for the future:

1. _____

For each skill listed, note each activity you've undertaken to maintain your skill (include company-sponsored training, seminars and conferences, meetings with a mentor, community college or university extension courses, 360-degree feedback, and other activities). Note the date of the activity; complete at least one activity every 60 days.

DATE   ACTIVITY

_____
_____
_____

TECHNOLOGY SKILLS
Computers, Software, and Any Technology Specific to Your Position

List two technology skills that you need in your current job:

1. _____
2. _____

List one technology skill to improve to better position you for the future:

1. _____

For each skill listed, note each activity you've undertaken to maintain your skill (include company-sponsored training, seminars and conferences, meetings with a mentor, community college or university extension courses, 360-degree feedback, and other activities). Note the date of the activity; complete at least one activity every 60 days.

DATE   ACTIVITY

_____
_____
_____

PEOPLE SKILLS
Managing People, Teamwork, Emotional Intelligence

List two people skills that you need in your current job:
1. _____
2. _____

List one people skill to improve to better position you for the future:
1. _____

For each skill listed, note each activity you've undertaken to maintain your skill (include company-sponsored training, seminars and conferences, meetings with a mentor, community college or university extension courses, 360-degree feedback, and other activities). Note the date of the activity; be sure to complete at least one activity every 60 days.

DATE   ACTIVITY

_____
_____
_____

JOB-SPECIFIC SKILLS
Any Skills Related Specifically to Your Job or Industry

List two job-specific skills that you need in your current job:
1. _____
2. _____

List one job-specific skill to improve to better position you for the future:
3. _____

For each skill listed, note each activity you've undertaken to maintain your skill (include company-sponsored training, seminars and conferences, meetings with a mentor, community college or university extension courses, 360-degree feedback, and other activities). Note the date of the activity; be sure to complete at least one activity every 60 days.

DATE   ACTIVITY

_____
_____
_____

copy'n clip

Figure 18.1 *After Sherman was laid off, we all got scared about our ability to compete in the job market. We created this form to keep us focused on maintaining our skills.*

food for thought

Gray's Notebook

1. *You invest in your 401(K), and you should invest in your own skills, too. Both investments are important in securing your future. Your goal should be to always keep yourself marketable. As we all know, there's really no such thing as job security anymore. Any of us could be looking for a job tomorrow. That's always a scary prospect, but it's less scary if you know you can compete with other candidates. (Looking for a new job doesn't have to be a negative thing, either—you may want to pursue a promotion in your current company.)*

2. *What specific actions can you take to become more effective and/or valuable at work? Most of us wait to be invited to learn something new, participate in a new project, or expand our roles. Don't wait! It's not up to your boss to make sure you continue to be valuable. Make it your responsibility to make yourself indispensable. Hone your skills, offer to lead new projects, even take on the tasks that no one else wants to do.*

3. *Stay up to date on the latest trends and current events in business and in your field. Subscribe to magazines in your field and make it a point to stock up at your local bookstore periodically. Look through community college catalogs for courses that can help you. Attend conferences and seminars. Network. See what's available from your company's training department and take advantage of what's offered. The more opportunities you give yourself to get information, the better.*

4. *Learn from your colleagues—and learn by helping them, too. Even if you can't get formal training, you can learn from your colleagues. Each one of them knows something you don't. Find out what it is. Volunteer to help teach others, too. Teaching helps reinforce your own learning and positions you as an expert in your organization.*

Addison's Brain Trust

Wait, there's more! Check out these books for additional information and insight:

The Fifth Discipline by Peter Senge (Currency, 1990)
Funky Business: Talent Makes Capital Dance by Jonas Ridderstrale and Kjell Nordstrom (Financial Times Prentice Hall, 2000)

S.P. Surfs the Internet

You're never too old. Check out these business icons and when they started the businesses that made them famous:

- ★ Ray Kroc started franchising McDonald's at 52
- ★ Ferdinand Graf von Zeppelin built his first airship at 61
- ★ Colonel Harland Sanders started Kentucky Fried Chicken at 62
- ★ Coco Chanel designed her famous women's suit at 71

Source: Daniel Yankelovich

Rick's Smart Talk

"If the only tool you have is a hammer, you tend to treat everything as if it were a nail."
—*Abraham Maslow*

Connie's Smart Questions

Sometimes people ask me how I learned English so quickly. First I tell them I am still learning. Then I tell them that learning is easier when you realize how many ways there are to learn. When I was learning English, for example, I watched TV, I read bus schedules, I read the signs in store windows, I listened to talk radio—I did everything I could think of. The same method can work for you. Ask yourself:

- Which company-sponsored training program can I sign up for?
- Will the company reimburse the cost of community college or online training programs?
- Who do I work with that can teach me a new skill?
- Is there a committee or task force I can volunteer for?
- Which books have I read lately? What books should I read?
- Which magazines or journals serve my profession or industry? What issues are they covering?
- What's happening in other industries that might be applicable to my company?
- What would I like to learn that isn't related at all to work?

Make a commitment to keep learning. Choose one thing to do each week—read an article, attend a seminar, or whatever—and then do it. Keep a record of what you do so that during your review you can show your boss what you're doing to improve your skills.

Gray's Anatomy of Business

When we interviewed Sherman for the creative job, he said something in the interview that really impressed me. He told us that he had 12 years of experience—not 1 year of experience 12 times. That was his way of telling us that he kept challenging himself and doing new things. I have to confess that before the reorganization I had 1 year of experience 12 times; since then, I feel like I've had another year of experience every 30 days. Make a list of the skills and expertise you can add to your tool kit to make you more valuable. Then do it.

Barbie's Brainy Glossary

Closure   The process of resolving our emotional response to events so that we can move forward. When breaking up with a boyfriend, it takes several weeks, although using ice cream accelerates the process.

Competitive advantage   Skills or expertise that give you a head start on other candidates when there are job openings.

Continuous personal improvement   Never being satisfied with your level of expertise or knowledge, and always seeking to do better.

Outsourcing   Assigning ongoing responsibility for a function to a person or firm outside the company.

chapter nineteen

Incompetence

How to Encourage—and Use—Feedback on Your Performance

Tiger Woods. Barbra Streisand. Toni Morrison. Bill Gates. Julia Roberts. Lance Armstrong. Would you describe each of them as competent? You would probably agree that all of them are far more than competent—they are all at the top of their game, better at what they do than perhaps anyone.

Now imagine Tiger Woods running Microsoft. Imagine Barbra Streisand on the golf course, and Julia Roberts racing in the Tour de France. Would you still describe them as competent? Would you rush out to see Bill Gates's new film or buy his new CD? Probably not. What happened? Nothing about any of these people changed at all. Only the context in which you were thinking about them changed. And that's the whole point.

Competence Is Not Absolute. It Exists Only in a Specific Context.

We tend to think of competence as a destination. I know I did. I remember when I got my first engineering job right out of college. I was so nervous those first few weeks. I was convinced that I didn't know anything, and worried that everyone else would figure that out in short order. I used to study the older guys (they were all guys then) and think, "I want to be good like they are, so I can relax." Over time, I did get good. And I relaxed. That was my mistake.

Chasing competence is a little like chasing the end of the rainbow: Every time you get close, it has moved further away. That's because competence is not a destination, it's a process. Being competent is finding a way to keep up with the change going on around us.

That's because change rarely just makes things different. It also makes them harder; the bar keeps getting raised. Consider an administrative assistant's job. Just the fact that we no longer use the word *secretary* tells you something. There was a time when a good secretary only needed to be able to take dictation and type. Today, an administrative assistant must be able to create and alter documents, maintain a database, do mail merge, create presentations, and much more. Just ask Noreen—she'll tell you exactly how demanding it is. All of us are doing more than our predecessors, so we can't relax. We have to keep up.

Your Career Depends on You Being Competent in the Right Context.

In the last chapter we talked about keeping your skills current. Isn't this the same thing? Not entirely. Yes, the ideas are related. But competence is how you use the skills you have, and how attuned you are to the cues you get about how to use them. That's where I really dropped the ball. I wasn't getting the cues at all.

In my mind, I was still doing the same job I had always done. I was coming to work and designing products. Everything else seemed situational, something I was doing until we got the division turned around and things went back to normal. But we weren't going back to normal. We were moving forward to a new normal, and I never thought about what competence would look like in that normal.

So I wasn't really just doing the same job, I was doing a new job. And everyone else was evaluating how I was doing in that new context. People were giving me feedback and I was trying to use it, but it was all very fragmented. When I look back, it's as if I was putting together a jigsaw puzzle. People would show me how two pieces fit together to make a corner, but I never had a sense of what the finished puzzle was supposed to look like.

Well, Virginia could sure see what the puzzle was supposed to look like. She never actually used the word *dumb* when she was talking to me, but I think she might have liked to. What Virginia saw that I did not is that when you begin to play a game, you have to play to win.

You Can't Move Forward in Half Measures.

I never thought in terms of shaking up my career. But when I took on some leadership responsibilities, there was no turning back. The alternatives were not pretty: I could go along being a so-so leader that no one took seriously or I could fail at leadership. Virginia saw that I should give it my best shot. That's why she was so blunt and let me know that I wasn't doing the bang-up job I thought I was doing.

She helped me see that the context had changed. What she expected of me changed. The only thing that hadn't changed was my expectations for myself. After our pep talk, that changed in a hurry.

Still, expectations are not a guarantee. You can't fail at something you aren't serious about anyway. But you *can* fail at something you really pursue. I didn't realize I was scared to fail, but I was. Ironically, my fear of failing was the thing that was getting me into trouble. In an effort not to fail, I was being safe—too safe.

I see now that there is no great success without great risk. I realized that I had to become competent at taking risks, and the only way to do that was to take them. Of all the things we faced after the reorganization, that was the hardest for me.

I've been the quintessential nice guy—easygoing, friendly, benign. I kept a low profile and stayed within my comfort zone. I saw that to succeed I was going to have to do things that would make me very uncomfortable. I was going to have to go out on a limb for something that not everyone agreed with. I was going to have to be willing to be wrong. I was going to have to risk being unpopular.

You Can't Be Truly Competent without Taking Risks.

Since this all started, I've done a lot of reading and studied a lot of leaders. I've decided that the only people who really succeed are the ones who are willing to venture outside their comfort zones. Have I done that? I'd say I'm a work in progress. Today I think I'm intermittently competent. I have good days and bad days. There are skills I'm still trying to develop. Some days I take risks and some days I don't. I think people see that I'm trying, but I think they wish I was more consistent.

I'm playing to win now. This I know for sure: If Lance Armstrong took up singing, he'd pursue competence with a vengeance.

performance review form

Employee Name: *Gray Blanderson*
Job Title: *Senior Product Designer*

Supervisor: *Virginia Edgarly*
Review Date: *November 30, 2000*

Design
☐ Exceeds Expectations
☐ Sometimes Meets Expectations

☒ Meets Expectations
☐ Does Not Meet Expectations

Comments: Gray's designs always deliver the functionality he's assigned. He also meets established budgets and I do wish that Gray showed more creativity. His work is solid but not exciting, and he has yet to suggest some designs of his own.

Teamwork
☐ Exceeds Expectations
☐ Sometimes Meets Expectations

☒ Meets Expectations
☐ Does Not Meet Expectations

Comments: Gray is very easy to work with. He is even-tempered and cooperative and positive. My sense is that Gray wants to be liked. I wish that Gray would be a more active team member. He doesn't take the opportunity to advocate for others or to intervene on their behalf. I compare Gray to a relay runner; he does what he needs to do, and then hands the baton to someone else. I'd prefer to be able to compare Gray to a basketball player working *with* them more directly.

Initiative
☐ Exceeds Expectations
☐ Sometimes Meets Expectations

☒ Meets Expectations
☐ Does Not Meet Expectations

Comments: I've been very pleased to see Gray take some initiative relative to his own development. On his own, Gray recognized that when he turned in work at the last minute it forced others on the team to scramble. He took it upon himself to allow more time for his work, and therefore to allow others more time for theirs. I wish that Gray were more aggressive on behalf of the division. Gray is not a risk taker; my sense is that Gray wants to know that whatever he does he can do well.

Decision Making
☐ Exceeds Expectations
☐ Sometimes Meets Expectations

☒ Meets Expectations
☐ Does Not Meet Expectations

Comments: Gray makes sound, timely decisions relative to his design work. Beyond that, however, he is less decisive. I don't think Gray avoids the responsibility of making decisions. I think he just doesn't want to make the wrong decision. If he wants more responsible positions, Gray will have to be more decisive.

Figure 19.1 *This is an excerpt from my performance review for the year before the reorganization. When I read it again, it really brought home how context defines our competence. I thought it was a good review; now I can see that Virginia was already commenting on my leadership and people skills.*

food for thought

Gray's Notebook

1. *Encourage feedback on your performance. Don't wait until your performance review. Instead, ask for feedback regularly. Start with your boss, but be sure to ask other people, too. Don't focus only on how you do tasks: Ask for feedback about your workplace politics, too.*
2. *Listen to people's suggestions on how you can do a better job. If you disagree, ask questions to better understand their point of view. Commit to improving.*
3. *Remember that competence is only relevant in context. If you take on a new project or move into a new job, you'll have to prove your competence all over again.*
4. *Building your competence may mean moving outside your comfort zone. Be prepared to do things you would prefer not to do. For example, developing competence in marketing may require making presentations. You may hate public speaking. Do it anyway.*

Addison's Brain Trust

Wait, there's more! Check out these books for additional information and insight:

The Age of Unreason by Charles Handy (Harvard Business Review, 1989)
Whistle While You Work: Heeding Your Life's Calling by Richard J. Leider and David A. Shapiro (Berrett-Koehler, 2001)

S.P. Surfs the Internet

Employee attitudes about work:

- ★ I'm given the information to do my job: 38% agree
- ★ I'm given the skills to do my job: 43% agree
- ★ I understand my company's goals: 83% agree
- ★ I understand my job's responsibilities: 87% of workers agree

Source: Watson Wyatt

Rick's Smart Talk

"No one can make you feel inferior without your consent."

—*Eleanor Roosevelt*

Connie's Smart Questions

When I was learning English, I told everyone I wanted them to correct me when I made a mistake. I meant it, too, even though I made a lot of mistakes. I figured I would never get better without the feedback—I'd just keep making the same mistakes. That's true no matter what you're doing. You need feedback. Ask yourself:

- Do you practice asking for feedback away from work with people who make you feel safe?
- Do you make it easy for people to decline to give you feedback or to put it off till another time?
- How do you convince people that you really want to hear what they have to say?
- Do you ask them to suggest how you could do a better job?
- Do you give them a chance to think about what they want to say?
- Are you careful to not to get defensive when someone is offering feedback?
- Do you take notes so you can refer later to what was said?
- Do you listen—really listen—to what they say?

Make a point of getting some feedback once a month. Choose different people to offer the feedback. Look for patterns in what they say. After a few months, meet again with people who've given you feedback. Find out whether they've seen improvement.

Gray's Anatomy of Business

I really believe in doing 360-degree evaluations. Getting feedback from the people above, below, and at the same level in the chain of command is so important. But I've got a way to get insight on how you are perceived that's more fun than a traditional 360. I call it the celebrity game. Choose the celebrity who best defines who you are at work. For example, if you are a good listener, you might choose Oprah Winfrey. Once you've chosen someone, ask the people you work with which celebrity they'd choose to represent you—and why they chose who they chose. Compare your choice to theirs.

Barbie's Brainy Glossary

Comfort zone   The range of activities that do not induce stress. Taking care of young children is outside my comfort zone.

Day spa   A facility offering massage, facials, and other services on an appointment basis. A really great place to go after you have ventured outside your comfort zone.

Midcourse correction   A change in direction or action after receiving feedback but before a project is completed.

Performance review   A formal assessment of your work. Theoretically valuable, but often done late and superficially.

chapter twenty

Withdrawal

How to Stay Focused on Your Mission and Connected to Others

The worst thing you can do to yourself and to your colleagues is to quit—and stay. I'm sure you've seen people do just that. They keep coming to work, occupying a desk, and collecting a paycheck. But they aren't really *there* anymore. Emotionally, they have moved on. They just haven't found the guts or the strength to quit.

You know the symptoms. They sit through meetings, but they don't contribute. They complain about a lot, but they do nothing to change things. They stop talking about the future because they don't think it's relevant. The pace of their work slows because they know if they finish one project they'll have to do another one—and they would rather not work that hard.

It's sad, really. Still, if they could withdraw without any penalties for the rest of us we could just shake our heads and ignore them. But there *are* penalties for the rest of us. They stop making any sort of real contribution, of course. Worse, they actually make doing our jobs harder because we end up working *around* them instead of *with* them.

When One Team Member Withdraws, the Whole Team Suffers.

One day I looked around the office and it seemed like half the team had withdrawn. Everyone except Sherman was still showing up, but no one's heart seemed to be in the work. I knew we'd never get the division back on track if we were giving it a halfhearted effort. What happened to everyone?

I don't want to sound mean, but everyone sounded like members of a 12-step program for whiners. This is what I was hearing: "They don't treat me with respect," "They aren't giving me the support I need," "They don't appreciate what I do," "They give me too much work to do," "They don't care what I think," and on and on and on. Sheesh. Does any of that sound familiar?

I can't let myself totally off the hook, either. I was whining about everyone else's whining. I found myself giving up too. One afternoon I just put my head on my desk and thought, "Who cares?" But some part of me did still care. I just didn't know what to do.

All the whining kept repeating like a song I couldn't get out of my head. Then the light bulb went off over my head (stuff like that happens in comics): they, they, they, they. Everyone was griping about what they weren't getting from someone else. Most often, "they" meant management, but sometimes it meant colleagues, too. Everyone was waiting for someone else to fix things.

It turns out I had been asking the wrong questions. People hadn't withdrawn from the job; they had withdrawn from themselves.

Our Engagement with Work Is Basically an Internal Matter.

Every day spent waiting for someone else to fix things is a day lost when we could have taken action ourselves. It's really a lost cause, too, because somebody else can't fix things.

If you think about it, it doesn't really make sense that we expect the boss to make us feel good about going to work. Remember back to your high school days. Your teachers gave you information and assignments, much as your boss does now. Your teachers also evaluated your work, just as your boss does now. But did you expect your teachers to also take care of your emotional needs? Of course not. You had friends, parents, maybe even siblings for that.

So why do we expect managers to take care of our emotional needs? (And let's not kid ourselves that we're not talking about emotional needs. We do have them—even at work. The needs to feel appreciated, supported, respected, and so on are wholly separate from the tasks at hand.)

I think it happens because—at least in our society—work is so much more than just a series of tasks, or even the source of a paycheck. Our work becomes our identity. When you meet someone new, isn't one of the first questions you ask, "What do you do?" Our jobs help define who we are for other people, so maybe it isn't surprising that jobs start to define us for ourselves, too.

You can see the evolution of our thinking: I have a job → my job defines who I am → my boss is in control of my job → my boss is in control of my identity → therefore, everything is my boss's responsibility. It's easy to follow. It's also wrong.

Our Work Often Defines Us, But It Doesn't Need To.

We are far happier when we define our relationship to our job instead of the other way around. But how do we do that? If it were obvious, I wouldn't have had so many unhappy coworkers.

Start by separating work tasks from your emotions. That's easier said than done. It may happen more readily at work, but we mix up emotions and tasks in other parts of our lives, too. (If you've ever had a fight about putting in a new roll of toilet paper or taking out the trash, you know what I mean.) It may not be easy, but it can be done—and it needs to be done.

Once you've isolated your emotions, you can look for ways to get what you need. For example, S.P. realized that she needed more support for the project she was working on. She was waiting for us to give it to her, but we couldn't—we didn't understand what she was doing well enough to help. But there were other places she could get it: peer groups, associations, or networking with people in other companies working on similar projects, for example. Finding the support she needed really energized her.

Sherman and Barbie each were contributing something unique, but each had lost sight of how they were contributing. They just needed to focus on the part of the work they had control over. In short, each person's way to engage is different.

Figure Out What You Need and Make It Happen—Don't Wait for Someone Else to Do It.

I've made it sound easy, and it isn't always easy. Some companies get in the way of you getting what you need. Some bosses are jerks. Some companies are so lean and mean that people have no personal lives left. In those cases, you may not be able to get what you need. If that's the case, then you may need to get out. But that's a decision you need to make, too. Quit and move on to something else. Or stay and give it your all. Just please don't quit and stay.

staying connected calendar

			1	2	3	4
			Send a news-paper article on a competitor		Use a personal note to remind them of an appointment with you	
5	6	7	8	9	10	11
	Surprise them with holiday greetings—for Labor Day			Send them a link to a Web site related to one of their hobbies		
12	13	14	15	16	17	18
		Send them a birthday greeting			Send them notice of a new law that could affect them	
19	20	21	22	23	24	25
	Send them an article on a different industry that may help them		Send a thank-you note for something they did			
26	27	28	29	30		
	Congratulate them on being mentioned in the media			Introduce them to a new potential customer		

copy'n clip

Figure 20.1 *Sometimes we all feel isolated, but it can be tough to find excuses to stay in touch with business colleagues. We brainstormed ideas and created this calendar to remind ourselves to follow through.*

n o r e e n ' s   l i n g o   b i n g o

	B	I	N	G	O
1	INTEGRATE PAGE	SAME	EMPOWERED	DOWNLOAD WITH LESS	MORE
2	TEAM PLAYER	BOTTOM LINE	HEADS UP	CASCADE	PROACTIVE
3	DELIVERABLE	SYNERGY	*Free*	CUSTOMER-FOCUSED	INITIATIVE
4	OPTIMIZE	PARADIGM	RIGHTSIZE	VALUE-ORIENTED	GOAL
5	REENGINEER	RESOURCES	TAKEAWAY	COMPETENCY	STRATEGY

Figure 20.2 *Noreen got so burned out, cynical, and withdrawn that she created this lingo bingo card to use in meetings. The fact she even thought of it showed how disengaged she was. Ultimately we all started using it—but in a different way. We used the card to keep track of how much lingo we were using—and if anyone got bingo we knew we had lost our way: We were more focused on talking than doing.*

food for thought

Gray's Notebook

1. *Seek people who can give you support and insight. Include the people you work with, but also consider your family and friends, professional colleagues at other firms, members of your church group or other social clubs, and experts (such as trainers or teachers).*

2. *Find excuses to stay in touch with people in your network on a regular basis. Without attention, your network will wither and die. E-mail or call people often. Have a purpose for each interaction.*

3. *Look for opportunities to help other people. Reaching out will renew your sense of purpose. It will also extend your network. Helping people may also give you insight about yourself—your skills, your interests, your aspirations, and so forth.*

4. *Your engagement with work is internal; no one else can make sure you are engaged. Look for meaning and interest. List all the things that engage you about your current job. If you're not engaged and can't figure out a way to recapture your enthusiasm, it may be time to search for another job.*

Addison's Brain Trust

Wait, there's more! Check out these books for additional information and insight:

> *The Beauty of the Beast* by Geoffrey Bellman (Berrett-Koehler, 2000)
> *A Stake in the Outcome* by Jack Stack (Currency, 2002)

S.P. Surfs the Internet

Which movie title best describes the leadership of your company?

- ★ *Braveheart:* 13%
- ★ *The Four Horsemen of the Apocalypse:* 28%
- ★ *The Good, The Bad & The Ugly:* 58%

Source: Workingwounded/ABCnews.com

Rick's Smart Talk

"Denial ain't just a river in Egypt."

—*Mark Twain*

Connie's Smart Questions

When I first started at Global Gadget I knew almost nothing about shipping. I mean, I could tell you how to ship furniture from Costa Rica, but not how to get gadgets to Phoenix overnight. To figure it out, I looked for help everywhere. I asked my contacts at all the shipping companies, but I also talked to our customers about what they wanted and to people in the warehouses at other companies in the area. By the time I figured it out I had a stack of business cards on my desk, and I still call the people on those cards: Someday I am going to need them again. You can be more effective at work, too, if you seek help from everywhere. Ask yourself:

- Do you write down important information about people on the backs of their cards so you'll remember who they are and what they know?
- Do you look for opportunities to stay in touch—such as sending people information they will find interesting?
- Do you monitor information about your industry through the newspaper, Web sites, industry associations, and so on?

Make at least one networking call each week. Before you make each call, identify one thing you will give the person you're calling—the date of an upcoming meeting he or she might find interesting, the name of a new book on a topic of interest, and so on. Also have in mind one thing you want to get from that person—another contact, some insight about how he or she does things, and so on. Keep a notebook to jot down what you learn.

Gray's Anatomy of Business

Once when Taupe was reading one of her self-help books she told me about random acts of kindness. When she said it, it reminded me of a time when my car was in the shop. Taupe was out of town and Mavis was busy, and I remember standing at a bus stop in the pouring rain. Then an acquaintance saw me and stopped to offer me a lift. That gesture meant so much. Everyone I know loves it when someone does him or her a favor, but few of us seek out those opportunities. Now I make it a game: I try to do someone a favor without even thinking about whether they might reciprocate.

Barbie's Brainy Glossary

Community   A group of people with common and especially professional interests.

Isolation   The state of being socially withdrawn or removed from the rest of a group.

Network   An extended group of people linked by a common person and used by that person for support and information.

Perp walk   To escort someone as if he or she is a criminal perpetrator; likely to shame the person in question.

chapter twenty-one

Dysfunction

How to Stay Grounded—and Work with Those Who Aren't

Which was more dysfunctional: your most recent family Thanksgiving dinner or your most recent department meeting? If your family is like most families—and your workplace is like most workplaces—you'll have a tough time choosing.

It's not an idle question, because many workplace teams are like families. We all grow up in a family structure, so that's what we know. Whether we're aware of it or not, when we get to the workplace we replicate that structure in some way. (Well, that's what Global Gadget's employee assistance plan counselor told me when I called her the day Noreen was walking through the office with a tourniquet around her arm and offering her blood.) For example, people who grew up in families that were always in a crisis often create crises.

The specifics aren't really important. What *is* important is to know that we go to work every day and carry our dysfunction with us. By now, you've read far enough to have observed some of our dysfunction. (You're in a great position, because it's always easier to see this stuff in others than it is in ourselves.) You can't have missed Noreen's martyr complex or her flair for the . . . dramatic. You've probably seen Addison's obsessive-compulsive need for order and Rick's arrogance. Maybe they remind you of people you work with or have worked with.

We All Take Our Dysfunction to Work Every Day.

There's a lot of dysfunction to deal with every day. But it's more than that. You see, groups tend to breed their own dysfunction. That is, the group itself is dysfunctional in some way. (I heard that from the employee assistance counselor, too.) The counselor told me about one group that was too analytical. Once, they were assigned to complete a team-building exercise. In the exercise they had a limited time in which to construct something. The team spent three-fourths of the allotted time debating whether they really had to construct the apparatus or if there might be a way around it. They concluded there was no way around it and then began working. Despite the delay, they finished on time and the apparatus worked better than most. The instructor said he had never seen anything like it.

Again, the specifics aren't really important. What *is* important is to know that we take our own dysfunction into a workplace that has its own dysfunction. Dysfunction meets dysfunction—it's a combustible combination. Sometimes I wonder that anything gets done at all.

At Work, Our Individual Dysfunction Meets Group Dysfunction.

Things get done because none of us is only our dysfunction—at least not most of the time. We bring skills, talent, education, energy, and intellect to what we do. We use all that to get our jobs done, or to excel in them.

As we mature, most of us discover our dysfunction. We make mistakes. We see ourselves repeating patterns. Other people begin to complain about our nuttiness. Confronted with our imperfections, we learn to manage them. It takes effort, though. Noreen told me once that for every smart-aleck comment that comes out of her mouth, there are three others that she censors. Sometimes when Rick is on the phone, I can see him struggling to remain polite if the client is being difficult.

Some of us have even learned how to *use* our dysfunction. For example, Addison channels his obsessive-compulsive nature into finance, which requires a fanatical attention to detail. Addison has turned something that could be a disadvantage (imagine him teaching kindergarten, for example!) into an advantage.

Sometimes we use our dysfunction in less direct ways, too. Noreen's "no one knows how hard I work" routine is pretty effective at discouraging people from asking her for help. Of course, sometimes we have to ask for her help, but her attitude does limit what we ask for. Her neurosis may not help the team much, but it does help her.

In the same way we learn to manage our own neuroses, we also learn to manage working with other people's dysfunction and to manage the team's dysfunction. Of course, we learn to work with some people better than others, but that shouldn't be a surprise. Anyone as precise as Addison working with someone as imprecise as Juan is bound not to be easy. Sometimes we learn to draw on other people's quirks. I know I can rely on Juan to help me get my head out of the details enough to see the bigger picture.

We Learn to Manage Our Neuroses—and Those of Our Colleagues.

There's a reason people use the phrase *emotional teeter-totter.* When things are going well, we're grounded and our neuroses are at bay. But when things aren't going well, our dysfunction becomes more pronounced. It begins to weigh us down, until the teeter-totter reverses position and we're no longer so grounded.

You've read far enough to have seen that, too. Remember what happened when Addison suggested that Noreen could take a class to improve her software skills? Or how Addison reacted to the notion that we should leave our dirty dishes in the sink? It's not that either situation by itself was too much. They became too much, however, in the context of all the change and stress we all faced.

For some reason, even when we admit our flaws, we never quite see them as clearly as others do. We're even less likely to see how we respond to stress. I don't want to spoil any surprises by giving away what happens in this chapter, but let's just say we all got a chance to see exactly how our neuroses seem to others.

   It wasn't a pleasant experience. Noreen says it aged her 12 years, but that's Noreen for you. Still, I'm not sorry we went through it. We learned a big lesson.

The Teams That Ultimately Win Are Those That Learn to Manage Their Dysfunction as Well during Crises as They Do the Rest of the Time.

We're still learning. But we've gotten much better, and we've gotten to the point where we can tease each other. I'll tell you this much: Our meetings are much less dysfunctional than Thanksgiving with my family.

training department

GLOBAL GADGET

STRATEGIES FOR COPING WITH DYSFUNCTION

If we're at all successful, we learn to manage our own dysfunctions (at least most of the time). But how about coping with other people's dysfunctions? On the left side of this page are some common dysfunctional personality traits. On the right side are some effective coping strategies. Which strategy would you match with which dysfunction?

DYSFUNCTION	COPING STRATEGY
1. Chip on the shoulder	A. If they are talented, try to tune it out; if they aren't, keep your distance
2. Know-it-all	B. Proceed with caution; it is a very dangerous game to play
3. Last-minute	C. Do their share of the work or find someone who can
4. By the book	D. Learn as many ways to say "thank you" as possible
5. Firing squad	E. Look for clues so you can identify them early; keep your distance
6. Incompetent	F. Give a phony deadline to buy yourself some wiggle room
7. Saboteur	G. Use these people like a focus group to learn about potential problems
8. Micromanager	H. Pump them for information; even though they may be annoying, they may have valuable insight
9. Gossip	I. Copy them on every e-mail you send or receive
10. Whiner	J. Ask questions to learn the source of their anger; address it if you can
11. Helping hand	K. Reframe your suggestions so they sound like an extension of an existing program

Answer Key: 1-J, 2-H, 3-F, 4-K, 5-G, 6-C, 7-E, 8-I, 9-B, 1-A, 11-D

Figure 21.1 *We saw that we had to be as good at managing our dysfunction during a crisis as we are every day; the training department gave us these strategies to help.*

food for thought

Gray's Notebook

1. *Monitor your own dysfunction and dysfunctional reactions at work. None of us is perfect, and sometimes even our strengths (such as a keen attention to detail) can be a problem when taken to the extreme. That's why we owe it to ourselves—and our coworkers—to pay attention to our own eccentricities and foibles. Don't let them get in the way of the work.*

2. *Be on the lookout for dysfunction in your organization, coworkers, and boss. We aren't perfect, and neither are the people we work with. What's more, organizations themselves can become dysfunctional. For example, an organization may be so risk averse that paralysis results and the organization stops moving forward. When that happens, the best thing you can do is model functional behavior. In that situation, take some risks yourself and encourage others to do the same.*

3. *Increase your flexibility. Be ready for anything. Dysfunction is often triggered by a disruption in the status quo. In today's workplace, however, the status quo is often disrupted. Work to become more flexible so that you can roll with the punches when priorities or schedules change.*

4. *Winning teams manage their dysfunction during crises as well as they do the rest of the time. When crises happen, pay particular attention to how individuals and the team react. Work to contain dysfunction.*

Addison's Brain Trust

Wait, there's more! Check out these books for additional information and insight:

The Anxious Organization by Jeffrey Miller (Facts on Demand, 2002)
What Leaders Really Do by John Kotter (Harvard Business Review, 1999)

S.P. Surfs the Internet

Things that should tell you something is wrong at work:

- ★ Communication is indirect
- ★ Conflicts are not stated openly
- ★ Corporate memory is lost or forgotten

- ★ The search for the cause of a problem is personalized
- ★ Inconsistent application of procedures is not challenged

Source: If It's Broken, You Can Fix It *by Tom E. Jones (Amacom, 1998)*

Rick's Smart Talk

"It is not the critic who counts, the credit belongs to the man who is actually in the arena. Who strives valiantly, who errs and comes short time and time again; and who, if he fails, at least fails while daring greatly. His place shall never be with those cold and timid souls who know neither victory nor defeat."
—*Theodore Roosevelt*

Connie's Smart Questions

The downside of our efforts to get better is that we sometimes dwell on the negative. We focus more on the problems than on what's working. For example, when Buzz expressed his frustration about the way we pack our product, that defined the warehouse for a while; that issue became 100 percent of who we are. People forgot that 99 percent of all shipments are error free and that most customers are happy. That happens in other ways throughout the organization, too. We see all politics as negative, and we see some people only in the worst light. Instead of harping on everything everyone does wrong, spend some time looking at what they do right. Ask yourself:

- ▓ What common ground do I share with people?
- ▓ What interests do we share?
- ▓ What goals do we have in common?
- ▓ What skills do they have that could help me?
- ▓ What skills do I have that could help them?
- ▓ What expertise do they have that could help me?
- ▓ What expertise do I have that could help them?
- ▓ What contacts do they have that could help me?
- ▓ What contacts do I have that could help them?
- ▓ How can I reach out to them?

Make it a point to pay compliments to people and to thank them for things they do on your behalf. They'll appreciate the recognition, and you'll be surprised how it will improve your own morale.

Gray's Anatomy of Business

I used to complain about the people that I work with. They all seemed to have lots of baggage. Sometimes, for example, Noreen makes me crazy with her martyr stuff. But one day over lunch she told me about a boss she had who used to pick on her in staff meetings and tell everyone that what she did was useless. It was such a sad story, and it made me realize that Noreen's martyr behavior is just her attempt to get some affirmation of her work. I try to remember that when I lose patience. When I put two and two together about Noreen, I realized *I* have baggage, too. My first boss at Global Gadget was a real micromanager—he wanted to see everything we were working on every day. I adapted to that style, and I think that's part of what's made it hard for me to take risks. What baggage do you bring to work? Look at your own job history—how have you been "trained" to behave? Talk to some trusted colleagues to see if they have any insights.

Barbie's Brainy Glossary

Coffee   The elixir of life in liquid form. Without it, 60 percent of the people in the office would not function. See also *air* and *water*.

Dysfunction   Impaired or abnormal functioning. All those personality quirks that make you want to run screaming from the office some days.

Enable   To provide with the means or opportunity. We enable Noreen's martyr complex when we decide against asking for her help with a project.

Functional   Emotionally healthy enough to show up for work each day, appear to be normal, and get work done.

chapter twenty-two

The Spirit of Innovation

How to Implement New Ideas and Build for the Future

Innovation and genius are not the same thing. When I finally figured that out, I found it very reassuring, because I felt a lot of pressure to be a genius. Certainly there is a lot of pressure to do something new. In business we're so obsessed with innovating that we've invented a new vocabulary for it: *outside the box, paradigm shift, reorganization,* and *change management,* just for starters.

To keep up with the Dow Joneses, companies announce innovative products, innovative marketing, innovative work flow, innovative staffing, and, in some cases, innovative accounting. Surely all that innovation could only come from a blaze of brainpower worthy of Einstein or Stephen Hawking, right?

Actually, no. For all our talk about innovation, there isn't much that's really all that new. I don't mean new in the sense of a radical discovery or a bold, original vision that changes how we see the world and opens up unimagined possibilities. The theory of relativity, splitting the atom, and mapping the human genome are truly new—that's genius.

I don't know about you, but new stain fighters, new ways to squeeze commercial time into network television, and new colors of ketchup haven't rocked my world. Those may all be innovations, but they are not genius. My son Kelly could have dreamed up green ketchup. That's my point, actually. Although many of us think of innovation as something other people do, in truth we all innovate. We are also likely to think of innovation as big leaps forward. In fact, innovation is an incremental improvement to something that already exists.

All of Us Can—and Should—Innovate.

Would you describe yourself as an innovator? I don't think any of us would have. Still, we were innovating—in some way—all the time. An innovation is simply a change, and we were constantly changing things in small ways. For example, Addison would assign new colors to his files, or Noreen would reformat meeting minutes. Who cares, right? Exactly. Those innovations added nothing to the business. They didn't move us forward at all.

Imagine how much better off we would be if instead of reorganizing files Addison had found a better way to bill clients or forecast income. Imagine how much more competitive we would have been had we figured out a way to cut our production time before we lost Kitchen Cartel's business. Imagine that instead of wasting time creating a DVD gadget no one was clamoring for, we had created a really popular new product. In other words, suppose we were really good at innovating.

The Challenge Is to Get Good at Innovating, So that You Can Routinely Add Value to the Business.

What would it look like to be really good at innovating? The clearest sign is that innovation would be less random and more directly related to business problems or opportunities. In addition, innovation would be better integrated into the culture, so that we would have avenues to test ideas. Finally, we would better evaluate our progress so that we could celebrate our successes and learn from our failures.

I'd like to say that we've gotten really good at innovating. I think we've gotten better at it, but we have a long way to go. We need more practice. Most of our innovations came late in our effort to reinvent the division. In retrospect, I think it had to be that way. Effective innovation takes focus and effort. We had to resolve some of our other issues first. We needed to define our goals, comprehend our market, understand our customers, and atone for the Seven Deadly Workplace Sins. Only then could we give innovation our full attention.

When we did give innovation our full attention, we innovated with a vengeance. You'll see that we started making changes to almost every aspect of our business. For the first time, though, our efforts all supported our goals. Not all our efforts worked (more on that in the next chapter). More worked than didn't, however, and I think we had gained confidence through some of our early successes. Remember when Connie found a way to deliver our gadgets to Buzz already unpacked? That taught us to look outside our division for ideas and expertise. It became easier to innovate when we had more brainpower to draw on and could learn from other perspectives. We also learned that the innovation is more powerful when it solves more than one problem.

Innovation Shouldn't Be Random. Focus Your Efforts on the Areas that Have the Greatest Impact on the Business.

With every success, innovation became more a part of our culture. We got better at supporting one another in our efforts. We got better at sharing information and at creating structure. Perhaps it sounds contradictory that something like innovation needs structure. I do think that too much structure can kill innovation, but you need some. We needed to establish milestones so that we made a point of checking our progress. We needed some structure to report back to each other. We needed to know which projects were our top priorities.

Those elements all became part of our pilot programs, in which we tested our ideas to see whether they would work. The pilots proved invaluable, because some ideas that sounded great on paper didn't really pan out. If we had followed our gut instincts alone, we would have spent a lot of time heading down dead-end streets. We had so little margin for error that we needed to know our efforts were wisely invested. The pilots helped us do that.

The very nature of pilots also forced us to evaluate our efforts. When they didn't work, everything we did was still fresh in our minds and we could evaluate what we learned. By focusing on learning, we were able to stop worrying about failure and blame and to focus on applying what we knew. We also started celebrating what we accomplished. Often we get so busy that we take our successes for granted. But they warrant a celebration to mark our achievements. We learned that lesson from Rick, who started ringing a bell to celebrate his big sales. The bell inspired the rest of us to score big successes, and that really pumped up morale.

Structure Helps Integrate Innovation into the Culture and Forces You to Learn from What You're Doing.

As the word *structure* implies, innovation is pretty methodical. Nothing we did was a radical departure from what many other businesses are doing, yet it made all the difference to our future. As I said, innovation is not genius. But innovating effectively? There may be genius in that.

m e m o

To: G. Blanderson, R. Newman, J. Del Toro, N. St. Mary, S. Fox, A. Applebaum, B. Falwell, C. Sanchez
From: S.P. Chang
CC:
Date: 09/03/01
Re: Just-in-Time

Hey Team:

Many people mistakenly believe that JIT is about automation. Actually, although JIT can describe a new production system, it's a philosophy of continuous improvement. The primary goal of JIT is to eliminate any waste or activity that doesn't add value, and in the process improve productivity. Most often, JIT focuses on eliminating seven kinds of waste:

1. Waste of waiting/idle time
2. Transportation waste
3. Processing waste
4. Waste from product defects
5. Inventory waste
6. Waste of motion
7. Waste from overproduction

I don't think we should focus our energies on all these things. To begin with, we don't have time. I also don't think it would be appropriate; according to the American Production and Inventory Control Society (APICS), the process can be applied to all parts of an organization (e.g., operations, distribution, sales, accounting). When JIT is used effectively, there are six benefits:

1. Reduced cost
2. Improved delivery
3. Improved quality
4. Added flexibility
5. Improved performance
6. Increased innovation

Beyond the support of all departments, JIT will also rely on trust and commitment between our customers and us. In truth, this calls for more than just selling product. It means that we need to establish partnerships with key customers. There are four cornerstones of this kind of partnership: trust, communication, a linear production system, and the time to make required changes.

Most manufacturing systems rely on meeting production schedules, cost projections, and product specifications. We're doing all that and still not winning. That's because we've missed two vital elements: making production as efficient as possible and meeting customer demands at the same time. To do that, here are some changes to consider:

· Moving decision-making to the line, reducing management's role but making employees more responsible and expanding their role beyond a single "job"
· Designing our products to meet customer requirements *and* production efficiency
· Requiring the sales staff to collect more information about what customers want
· Creating a quality assurance function
· Establishing performance measures, and then reporting on our progress against those measures to the whole division
· Involving suppliers in the early stages of product development
· Increasing the frequency of product delivery

Obviously, this is a lot. We can't do it all, certainly not right away. But there may be elements we can begin to use right away to turn the division around. In any case, we need to get together and talk about all this. Let's schedule a JELL-O attack ASAP.

Figure 22.1 *This is the memo S.P. drafted to summarize JIT for us. Obviously, we didn't use all these ideas, but the concepts were central to what we did.*

food for thought

Gray's Notebook

1. *Create a pilot program to test your idea on a small scale. No company can afford to squander time and money on ideas that don't pan out. But healthy companies explore as many ideas as possible. That's why pilots are so important. They allow companies to test many ideas in a low-risk way, and they allow employees to work out the bugs in any innovation before implementing it. Make sure you set up a pilot that will give you enough information to let you know whether you should proceed.*

2. *Collaborate with other people from other disciplines. Innovation is never a miracle from on high. Instead, it is the effective fusion of several ideas. The more ideas you have to draw on, the more likely it is that your idea will be a strong one. Seek out people who have expertise you lack. To figure out the financial implications of your idea, for example, work with a financial expert.*

3. *Don't fall in love with your first idea—be open to the second right answer. Most innovation is an iterative process, so your first idea may be the first necessary step and not the final answer. Don't view early setbacks as failures. Instead, apply the lessons from your first try to later attempts.*

4. *Celebrate your successes. Innovation is worth celebrating. Take time to mark your accomplishments. Help to create a culture that values innovation. Make a special effort to recap how your risks paid off.*

Addison's Brain Trust

Wait, there's more! Check out these books for additional information and insight:

> *Intrapreneuring in Action: A Handbook for Business Innovation* by Gifford Pinchot and Ron Pellman (Berrett-Koehler, 1999)
> *Please Don't Just Do What I Tell You* by Bob Nelson (Hyperion, 2001)

S.P. Surfs the Internet

The 10 Commandments of Innovation:

1. *Remember, it is easier to ask for forgiveness than for permission.*
2. *Do any job needed to make your project work, regardless of your job description.*

3. *Come to work each day willing to be fired.*
4. *Recruit a strong team.*
5. *Ask for advice before resources.*
6. *Forget pride of authorship; spread credit widely.*
7. *When you bend the rules, keep the best interests of the company and its customers in mind.*
8. *Honor your sponsors.*
9. *Underpromise and overdeliver.*
10. *Be true to your goals, but realistic about ways to achieve them.*

Source: Intrapreneuring in Action: A Handbook for Business Innovation *by Gifford Pinchot and Ron Pellman (Berrett-Koehler, 1999)*

Rick's Smart Talk

"You have to kiss a lot of frogs to find a prince."   —*Catchphrase often heard at 3M*

Connie's Smart Questions

Innovation is risky business. But playing it safe is more risky. That's what I learned through our reorganization. No one had done anything new and different in the Appliance Division for several years, and the result is that we nearly disappeared. The world is changing so fast that we have to change with it. Ask yourself:

- Is there something that could be done that would raise more revenue?
- Is there anything you can do to cut costs?
- What opportunities is your company overlooking?
- Who would directly benefit from whatever change you propose? How can you make contact with these people or departments?
- Who else wins if your innovation succeeds? How can you enlist them to support your cause?
- What can you learn from past change initiatives?
- Who will oppose new ideas?
- How can you win the support of change resistors, or at least get them to not actively oppose what you are trying to do?
- How can you measure the improvement your change has generated?

Get in the habit of taking risks. Do something risky at least once a week. (Remember, risky and reckless are not the same thing.) Start out taking small risks if that's easier, but take them regularly. Make a point of noting how your risks pay off. Support others in their risk taking.

Gray's Anatomy of Business

This exercise isn't as morbid as it sounds. Write your obituary. Really. Think of all the things that you would like to have accomplished while you were alive. Would your obit be full of accomplishments, or would it say things like, "I could have achieved great things if it weren't for my boss getting in my way," or "My colleagues undercut my efforts"? Focus on the things you should be doing and come up with a plan to do them. Would you rather have an obituary full of could'ves and would'ves?

Barbie's Brainy Glossary

Innovation   A new idea, method, or product. Colored ketchup is an innovation.

Intrapreneur   One who forges change with an entrepreneurial zeal from within.

JELL-O® attack   A soft response to a crisis (such as having a meeting or forming a task force) that conveys the appearance of taking action without really accomplishing much.

Pilot program   A focused test of a new idea to see whether it is viable and to uncover any glitches so that they can be corrected before rollout.

chapter twenty-three

Obstacles to Innovation

How to Overcome the Roadblocks to Success

Innovation isn't easy or perfect. If it were, your computer wouldn't crash so often. By its nature, innovation is usually an incremental change. Because the change happens in inches, not miles, some flaws are bound to remain. For example, I find that there are still things that my word processing program does (or won't do) that make no sense. Still, it's better than what's come before.

The slow pace of innovation is not the only challenge we face in making change. We're forced into trial-and-error learning because we don't have enough information, we don't have control of all facets of the process, or we aren't asking the right questions. At first, I thought all these speed bumps meant that we had rushed ahead testing ideas too soon. I thought we hadn't done our homework and that therefore we were wasting our time.

In retrospect, I've decided I was wrong. There wasn't any more preparation to do because we didn't know what we didn't know. A few years back, I watched a series about the space program called *From the Earth to the Moon*. In one episode, scientists were talking about how to solve the problem of getting a rocket to the moon and back. One scientist pointed out that the first challenge was to solve the problem of getting a rocket into space; only then would they know the questions to ask for the next step. I wish I'd remembered that during our process. I would have been more patient.

Accept that Innovation Is a Trial-and-Error Process.

You can't be innovative without exploring every possibility. That's why information is so important: It can help you figure out which avenues to pursue and how to pursue them. Our exploration of Just-in-Time principles is a good example. S.P. first raised the idea that the techniques could help us only a couple of days after Virginia first announced the reorganization. Then months passed in which all we did was mention the subject once in a while. We didn't know where to begin. Only after S.P. did some research did she see that we could apply some of the principles to our work flow. In that situation, we were literally helpless without the information.

You're still pretty helpless, actually, until you do a pilot. S.P. had some ideas for changing our work flow, but that's all they were: ideas. We had no way of knowing whether they would work because we had no experience against which to judge them. I compare the process to driving. Most novice drivers are pretty sloppy: They stop too close to the cars in front of them (if they stop in time), and they take corners too fast. That's because they have no frame of reference. Ask them if they are applying the brake soon enough and they can only think, "Compared to what?" Ask the same question of an experienced driver. They know whether they are braking soon enough because they've used the brakes thousands of time before and they can accurately predict what will happen.

None of us could predict what would happen, so we had to do a pilot—several pilots, actually. Each time, we had to see what happened when we made changes and then (and this is key) adjust accordingly. S.P.'s pilot was a great success. Juan and Connie, however, ran into trouble trying to forge new partnerships with vendors. Each time we learned more about what the vendors were thinking: They were afraid of sharing their business strategy, afraid of losing control of the partnership, afraid we would realize more value than they did. The information we gained has been a real help in shaping the offers we take to our vendors, but we're still struggling to make the relationship work well.

Information is vital. But a word to the wise: A little information can be a dangerous thing. In some cases, we knew just enough to pursue an idea but not enough to do it well. Addison's focus on cutting defects is a good example. S.P.'s research told us that reducing product defects should pay off. In most instances, I'm sure that's true. But Addison spent a lot of time pursuing an idea that he later said he shouldn't have pursued. For one thing, we should have known what our defect rate was, and we didn't. But the real issue is that so many of our products are so inexpensive to produce that correcting the few defects in each batch would cost more than we could recoup. In 20/20 hindsight, it makes sense: Correcting defects in cars yields big savings; in gadgets, not so much.

Information Is Vital. But Make Sure You Have Enough Information to Proceed.

It's great when innovation can happen in a vacuum—when you have total control. Unfortunately, in some cases others have a vested interest in the outcome. For example, many innovations in movie making depend on cooperation from the theaters. Sometimes theater owners have embraced those changes (widescreen images, surround sound) and sometimes they have not (3D and Smell-O-Vision). As I've mentioned, we ran into that problem trying to work with our vendors.

When this happens, the best thing to do is to temporarily abandon your innovation mode. Instead, revert to your sales mode and go about countering objections. Of course, both modes demand information and involve asking a lot of questions. But when innovating, most questions are internal; in sales, they are external. In your sales mode, get enough information so that you can answer concerns and show your partners how they benefit. If we had been truly compelling in presenting a win-win scenario, we would have had better luck. We sometimes forgot our sales lessons and focused too much on the benefits to us.

If Your Innovation Depends on a Partner, Don't Forget Your Sales Techniques.

We focused our energy on many areas before we ever got to one of our best ideas. That's because we weren't asking ourselves the right question. We kept asking, "What can we do that's new?" without asking, "What can we do better?"

"What can we do better?" was implicit in what we were pursuing. But we needed to make it explicit. We needed to challenge everything, not just the obvious problems. Only then could we really be open to seeing things in a new way. As you'll see, that idea paid off most right on my own desk. I took my focus off each individual task and expanded it to the whole. That allowed me to find the common denominators in my work, which in turn allowed me to make changes that affected numerous tasks all at once. The pace of our innovating really improved.

Question Everything You're Doing and Ask What You Can Do Better.

We're coming to the end of our story—so far. It's been quite a journey, often painful but also often thrilling. Our turnaround effort was a lot like adolescence: I'm glad I went through it, but I'm not eager to do it again.

We aren't done. Our work, like my computer, still crashes sometimes. But, also like my computer, it's better than anything else out there. That's far more than I could have dared dream when Virginia first told us we had six months to prove our value. We did it, together. We did it—and so can you.

m e m o

To: All Staff, Small Appliance Division
From: Virginia Edgarly
CC: M. Wellington Wadsworth, CEO
Date: 10/12/01
Re: New Appointment

Let me begin by saying that I am most impressed with all that you have accomplished in a few short months. Candidly, I did not think this division could be saved. This is one instance in which I am happy to be proven wrong.

From the moment I announced the reorganization, Gray Blanderson has stepped forward to lead the turnaround effort. No one asked Gray to do this. He saw the situation for the crisis that it was and refused to concede defeat. He has stepped forward to lead even while continuing to fulfill his regular job duties. It has not been easy for him. He has faced blunt criticism from many people, including me. He has made some very public mistakes and has had to learn many things very quickly.

Since your win on *Darwin's Desk,* I have seen Gray take another leap forward. He has been willing to take risks, something that clearly is outside his comfort zone. I think venturing outside one's comfort zone is the greatest challenge there is, and I admire Gray's willingness to do it. In doing so, he also has helped you all overcome the obstacles to innovation. He has been willing to accept failure and learn from it. He also has overseen pilot programs in which you worked out the flaws in some new ideas. Most of all, he has been able to look at his own job and see it a new way, reinventing his own work process and making it possible to greatly improve our delivery time. It is not easy to look at oneself in the mirror and challenge the basic fabric of one's job.

Through all this, Gray has earned your respect. Therefore, I'm sure that you will be pleased to know that effective immediately Gray has been named general manager of the Small Appliance Division. In this new capacity, Gray will be responsible for the day-to-day operation of the division and for meeting the division's business goals. All of you will now report to Gray.

Some specifics of the job are still being worked out. Gray will continue to report to me. I look forward to working with him. Please join me in congratulating Gray.

Figure 23.1 *Virginia's memo announcing my promotion. I have it framed in my office.*

food for thought

Gray's Notebook

1. *Obstacles happen. Accept that they are part of the innovation process. There are loose pavers on every yellow brick road. Don't stand in the road cursing at them and refusing to go on. Step over them or go around them, but keep moving.*

2. *Learn what you can from obstacles and mistakes. Setbacks and mistakes are only tragic if you don't learn from them. Make a note of what you learn and apply it.*

3. *Find out how others have overcome obstacles. The obstacle you face seems unique; it isn't. Somebody somewhere has faced it before. Do some research to find out who has faced the obstacle previously; learn from their experiences.*

4. *The biggest obstacle may be success. We all know the adage, "If it ain't broke, don't fix it." There's certainly some truth in that. But that idea can also hinder us. That's because when we are looking to make a change or improvement, we often ignore the things that are working best. However, sometimes those things need to be changed, too. For example, film director M. Night Shyamalan (he made* The Sixth Sense *and* Signs*) says that his favorite scene always ends up on the cutting room floor because the overall movie is better without it. Don't be afraid to let go of your favorite scenes.*

Addison's Brain Trust

Wait, there's more! Check out these books for additional information and insight:

> *Out of the Crisis* by Edwards Deming (MIT, 1986)
> *Stewardship* by Peter Block (Berrett-Koehler, 1996)

S.P. Surfs the Internet

How things *really* get done at work:

- ★ Grieve, counter, befuddle, and quit
- ★ Blame, hide, wait, and go home
- ★ Organize, label, date, and file
- ★ Deny, resist, explore opportunities, and accept

Source: Managing for Dummies *by Bob Nelson and Peter Economy (IDG, 1996)*

Rick's Smart Talk

"Do not let your obstacles master you, rather you become the master of your obstacles."
—*Helen Keller*

Connie's Smart Questions

I don't believe in fair fights. I want to get as many people and ideas on my side as possible so that that the first thing I see is the victory flag. Ask yourself:

- Whose palm can you grease?
- What secrets can you share?
- What questions can you ask?
- What can you try that hasn't been tried before?
- What shouldn't you do?
- How can you make tackling an obstacle more fun?
- Who hasn't been given a chance to help?

Choose an idea you've wanted to try for some time. Write it down. Now, go through and ask yourself all these questions relative to your idea. Once you've come up with the answers, introduce your idea. You can't have any excuses left.

Gray's Anatomy of Business

Obstacles. Wouldn't life be sweet without them? What am I saying? Obstacles are what gives life its challenge, its sense of accomplishment, its reward. Obstacles are part of the process. As long as you plan for them, they can be a great learning experience. They can also help ensure the long-term success of whatever you are trying to accomplish. Write down some of the obstacles you currently are facing. Talk to people to find out what creative solutions that they've found to address these or similar obstacles.

Barbie's Brainy Glossary

Ally   A person who supports your work or cause.

Golf   A male bonding activity, during which everything really important happens. Also a great excuse for a country club with good food and better parties.

Obstacle   An impediment to progress or achievement.

Tipping point   The point at which momentum of some sort reaches critical mass and change begins. For us, the tipping point in our turnaround came when Gray thought about identical product designs.